T0108388

Japanese Jewels

JAPANESE JEWELS

Ron Heywood

Foreword by
Patricia St John

Lutterworth Press
Cambridge

Lutterworth Press
P.O. Box 60
Cambridge CB1 2NT

British Library Cataloguing in Publication Data
Heywood, Ron
     Japanese jewels.
     1. Japan. Christian church. Evangelism. -
     Biographies - Collections
     I. Title
     269'.2'0922

ISBN 0-7188-2784-8

First published by Lutterworth Press 1989

Printed and bound in Great Britain by
The Guernsey Press Co. Ltd., Guernsey, Channel Islands.

CONTENTS

Foreword by Patricia St John   7
Introduction   9

 1. The pastor at suicide cliffs   13
 2. The grandmother who became an intercessor   23
 3. The gangster whom Christ arrested   27
 4. The maid who built a church   31
 5. Is there life after death?   37
 6. The man who honoured the Lord's Day   43
 7. The proud mayor who was humbled   49
 8. Thankful for TB!   55
 9. Prayer that recovered a plough   61
10. The gambler at wits' end corner   67
11. The film star who failed   75
12. The young organist and her problem son   81
13. Through trials to triumph   85
14. She dreamed of the Lord's return   93
15. A stormy tent mission and the aftermath   101
16. The wife of a condemned war criminal   109
17. From stonemason's son to bible college principal 117

Foreword

Miss Lilias Trotter, who went out to Algeria in 1888 and worked among Moslems for forty years, wrote the following words:

> A lesson I have learned through the stress of earthly warfare is the principle of the intense importance, on the parallel lines of the unseen strife, of consolidating victory. No gain is counted gain to those on the fighting lines, till it has come through the counter-attacks that invariably dog the steps of every forward move. It is not the flush of triumph in gaining a position, but the ability to hold it when it is challenged afresh, that determines ultimate victory or defeat.

For this reason I believe that this book will be of special interest for those who have worked for God and seen men and women coming to Christ. These characters have come through the counter-attacks and grown to Christian maturity. They have learned, through the tests and joys and sorrows of life, to know God. We can leave them with their feet set firmly on the Rock.

Each chapter gives the history of an individual, and these individuals vary widely in age and background and experience; the only thing they have in common is their tenacity and the fact that, against great odds, they battled through. In these days, when millions hear the Gospel on television and radio and through mass evangelism, many respond, but many turn back because the way is too hard or the price too high; also, perhaps, because those who lead them on and shepherd them through are few and far between.

But in this book we keep catching glimpses in the background of those who came alongside these converts, taught them, listened to them, loved them, and prayed them through. Just as the Saviour left the flock to seek for one sheep so these stories highlight the potential worth of one soul - even the soul of a little old woman - in terms of what it may become in the kingdom of God.

I have lived among Moslems for many years where the sharing of the Gospel in any real sense is almost always with individuals, and reading this book encouraged me tremendously. I believe that it will encourage many others and will also move us to pray for those about whom it was written, most of whom are probably still alive. I warmly commend this book.

PATRICIA ST JOHN

Introduction

'Japanese jewels?' did you say. 'Cars, motor-bikes, cameras, TV sets and other electronic equipment, yes, but I never associated Japan with jewellery, apart from pearls.' Japan has certainly led the world in the production of cultured pearls but in this book you will be introduced to other rare gems that I discovered in the land of the rising sun.

The Japanese perfected a method of growing cultured pearls towards the end of the nineteenth century and they held a monopoly of the trade during the early decades of the twentieth century. The process was invented by Kokichi Mikimoto. An irritant is introduced into the oyster which secretes layers of nacre which slowly cover the irritant and grow into a pearl. The process takes from one to four years, depending on the size of the pearls. Only a small proportion of the pearls are of marketable quality.

Jewels have been admired and appreciated from earliest times. They have adorned wealthy monarchs and beautiful women alike. Throughout the scriptures we find references to jewels and precious stones. Did not Abraham's servant give Rebekah 'gold and silver jewellery' (Gen. 24:53)? The breastpiece of the high priest's garment had four rows of precious stones on it (Exo. 28:15-17). The wall of the Holy City is to be made of jasper and the foundations are to be decorated with every kind of precious stone (Rev. 21:18-19).

One of London's main tourist attractions is the Tower of London. It is there that the Crown Jewels are housed and who could estimate the value of that collection? 'Atop the gold sceptre flashes the enormous Star of Africa, a flawless diamond, 516½ carats in all: the largest stone cut from the largest diamond ever yet found, the three thousand carat Cullinan, which was discovered in South Africa and presented to Edward VII by the South African Government. It was cut into nine huge diamonds and dozens of brilliants, and the largest of the nine stones added to the sceptre as a declaration of the power and wealth of the monarchy .... The crown used in the coronation ceremonies is called St Edward's Crown, and was made in 1662 for Charles II .... It is set with four hundred and forty gemstones, and weighs over seven pounds.' (*Jewellery* by Nancy Armstrong p. 139).

Another famous jewel is the Koh-i-Noor diamond. It came from India. The Governor-General of India sent it to Queen Victoria after the conquest of the Punjab. It was set in the crown which Queen Mary wore at the Coronation of George V and again in the crown made for Queen Elizabeth, wife of King George VI.

A perennial problem that perplexes travellers to other countries is that of selecting suitable presents for friends and relatives. It was somewhat easier in the days of travelling by sea for there was not the same restriction as regards weight. Air travel, however, poses the problem of keeping within the 20 kilograms allowance. The primary considerations are usually price and weight!

The problem came up for discussion when I was being entertained in the manse of Doveton Baptist Church, Victoria, Australia, by the Rev. and Mrs John Evans. Ladies are often better at selecting presents and it was Mrs Evans who suggested buying some inexpensive opals from the Lightning Ridge Opal Mines shop in the centre of Melbourne. As I entered the shop, one of the assistants informed me that they were about to show a video of the mining of opals. 'Would you like to see it?' he enquired. Coffee was served during the showing of the film, making me increasingly apprehensive about the pressurised salesmanship! One thing that I did learn was that, after unearthing a ton of earth and stones, they were lucky if they found as much as a handful of opals.

It has been rather like that with missionary work in Japan. Many tracts may be distributed but it is only the odd one that unearths a jewel. Many a sermon may be preached without any evident response. Many homes may be visited and seemingly the time has been wasted. Yet, as one looks back and looks around, one sees many precious jewels gleaming in the light shed upon them by the Son of Righteousness. Often they have been unearthed from the most unlikely soil. In the course of the next few pages, let me introduce some of them to you.

JAPAN

Hokkaido

Honshu

Fukushima ●

Shirakawa ●

Otawara ●

Tochigi ●

Kashiwa ●

Tokyo ●

Numazu ●

Obama ● Nagoya ●

Yoka ● Kyoto ●

Kashiwara

Akashi Kobe ● Osaka ●

Nara ●

Okayama ● Shodo ● Myoji ●

Oasa ● Shirahama ●

Susami ● Kushimoto ●

Shikoku

Uwajima ●

Kyushu

1:10,000,000

100   50   0   50   100   150   200 miles
       100   0   100   200   300   km

Jewel No 1

The Pastor at Suicide Cliffs

The Emi family had for 300 years provided the priest for the Buddhist temple of a small town in Okayama prefecture. Young Taro's main playground as a child was the precincts of the temple of which his grandfather was the priest in charge. His father having died while still quite young, the expectation of the family was that Taro would one day assume grandfather's mantle.

On a wet day when grandfather was away Taro and his friends were playing hide and seek inside the temple building. Having been spotted by one of his friends, Taro tried to escape by grabbing hold of the arm of an ancient wooden idol to swing himself clear of his pursuer. Unfortunately for him the wood had partly rotted and was unable to bear his weight with the result that he found himself sprawled on the floor clutching the arm of the idol!

It was a very valuable idol and his grandfather was livid with anger when he discovered what Taro had done. What he said would be better not printed but suffice it to say the grandson received the hiding of his life! A sore posterior gave Taro cause to reflect on what had happened. He reasoned to himself that if the idol was really a god then he should have been able to defend himself against a young schoolboy. The seeds of doubt concerning his grandfather's beliefs had been sown in a child's heart.

It was when he was a teenager that Taro first attended a Christian service and it was such a contrast to the cold formal incomprehensible prayers that his grandfather uttered daily in the temple that, like John Wesley of old, he found his heart strangely warmed. He began to attend the services regularly and took a delight in putting difficult questions to the pastor. These were often hard to answer, so much so that the pastor found himself hoping that he would stop coming because of the disruptive influence on other young members of his congregation. It was the message of love, the story of the cross, which softened his heart and dispelled his arguments. He came to believe that Jesus Christ was indeed the Son of God and he was overwhelmed by the realisation that Jesus had loved him enough to die in his stead.

It was no easy matter, however, for him to become a committed Christian for there was his family to consider. What would be their reaction to his becoming a Christian? Were they not expecting him to succeed his grandfather and maintain the family tradition? Was it right for him to hurt them and disappoint them in this way? It was a difficult decision for a young fatherless boy, but he knew in his heart that he could never become a Buddhist priest. How could he if he believed in Jesus Christ? It took great courage on his part to make known to his family his decision and he rehearsed to himself over and over again what he would say to them in order to cause the least hurt. As anticipated, however, they were horrified and did all they could to discourage him from attending any further Christian services without actually forbidding him to go, for it was a time of uncertainty for many of the Japanese people. Under the recently concluded peace treaty Japan had promised freedom of religion, and, as a consequence, some people did not know what attitude to adopt.

A greater shock awaited the family a few years later, for somewhat nervously Taro announced his intention of going to the Japan Evangelistic Band (JEB) Bible College at Kobe the following April to train to become a full-time Christian worker! It came like a bombshell to them and at first they were stunned by his disclosure, but they quickly regained their composure and advanced every conceivable argument in an endeavour to persuade him to change his mind. Did he not care about their reputation and the disgrace this would bring to the family? They would be ashamed to go out in the streets in this small town where everyone knew them. Was he not aware that the Emi family had provided a priest for the temple with an unbroken chain extending back more than 300 years? It was bad enough his becoming a Christian but a full time Christian worker was another matter - that was going too far.

They failed to deflect the young man from doing what he believed to be the will of God and, after completing four years of study, he graduated and joined the JEB. He was appointed to assist me in the pioneer work of church planting at the small town of Susami in Wakayama prefecture, to which I had gone some five months earlier. To be honest I don't think I ever had a Japanese co-worker who caused me so many problems! He was, of course, at that time only 22 years of age and had been admitted to the bible college at an exceptionally young age, so that he lacked experience and was somewhat immature. Time keeping, so essential to a Christian worker, was not his strong point and we had some problems over that. Then too he was really too handsome for his own good, so there were difficulties for him in his relationship with the young ladies who came to our services - not that he was ever guilty of immoral conduct.

Some years later he left the JEB after accepting a call to become the pastor of Shirahama Baptist church. Shirahama has become one of Japan's most popular resorts and at weekends the trains are packed with people taking a short break. It has a beach of lovely golden sands with very beautiful coastal scenery, making it a first choice for many honeymoon couples. In recent years hotels have sprung up like mushrooms for it is not far distant from either Osaka or Nagoya, which are Japan's second and third largest cities. It can be reached by train, boat, plane, bus or car. Representatives of the main hotels will be at the station to welcome the tourists, many of whom will have come in large parties for it is a favourite venue for company outings. They can be seen following the flag-waving representative to the waiting buses and cars. The majority have come on a short break to enjoy themselves, but some have come with heavy hearts and with a very different motive. They have come to end it all by jumping from Shirahama's suicide cliffs! In spite of prosperity and success Japan has a very high suicide rate of about seventy-five people per day. By dint of hard work Japan has risen to the very pinnacle of financial success and today her people enjoy a high standard of living, but has it brought satisfaction and happiness? The suicide statistics would suggest that the human heart craves something more than materialism can offer.

It was as a young bible college student that Mr Taro Emi first visited Shirahama. At that time one thing above all else had made a big impression on him: an inscription that he had read on one of the rocks at the head of the high cliffs - a memorial to a young couple who together had jumped to their deaths. They had fallen in love and longed to get married, but their parents had refused to give their consent. Mr Emi could not erase from his mind the thought of the wasted lives of these two young people and he wondered whether things might have turned out very differently if only they had heard the gospel of the Lord Jesus Christ.

By what seemed more than just a coincidence a dozen or more years later he received a call to become pastor of the Baptist church in that same town of Shirahama. As he thought back upon that earlier visit, he went once again to suicide cliffs and very cautiously advanced to the very edge. It was frightening even to look down at the sea below from that height and, on making enquiries, he discovered that there had been numerous other fatalities at that very spot. It was a very pensive pastor who slowly made his way home again, asking himself whether there was anything that he could do to help avert these frequent tragedies. As a first step he decided to approach the local authorities and obtained permission to erect a notice board at the top of the cliffs, on which were written words warning people that they only had one life to live and appealing to them not to throw it away. If they had problems or difficulties, they were invited to consult him and at the bottom of the notice board were his name, address and phone number.

The local telephone exchange became interested in this and erected nearby a telephone booth, making it easier to contact the church. Beside the telephone booth they put up a second notice board identical to the one at the top of the cliffs and, instead of dialling all of the numbers, contact could be made with the church by just pressing three buttons. The Shirahama branch of the Rotarians presented Mr Emi with an electronic device which enabled him to pick up messages that may have come to the church during his absence. The police are grateful for his co-operation and apparently the number of suicides at Shirahama has been reduced by 50 per cent.

An urgent call came to the church one day. Quickly putting

down the phone, Mr Emi leapt into his car and raced along the toll road that led to 'suicide cliffs'. The man at the toll gate, sensing the urgency, waved him past and on arrival he found two men and two children. Separating himself from the little group, one man ran quickly towards Mr Emi, saying 'Thank you for coming so quickly. That man over there and those two children were about to jump over the cliffs but I managed to stop them. I drew the father's attention to your notice board and asked if he would talk with you if I phoned. He promised to wait until you arrived.' After exchanging formal greetings the man informed Mr Emi that he had been deserted by his wife who had gone off with another man. Finding it impossible to hold down his job and also look after two small children, he had come to the conclusion that a family suicide was the only solution. Without telling his children what he had in mind, he had merely told them that he was going to give them a special treat and take them to Shirahama. They had excitedly boarded the train at Tennoji which followed along the coast for a large part of the journey. After the big industrial city of Osaka, it was a joy to them to see the farmers working in the paddy fields and then the beautiful blue of the sea. On arrival at Shirahama station they travelled by bus to the town and the beach. Children need little entertaining if they can swim and play on a lovely beach like Shirahama. 'Aren't you children hungry?' asked the father. 'Come on, get yourselves dressed and we will go and get something to eat.' He took them to a restaurant and let them choose whatever they wanted. 'After a meal like that you need a good walk. Let's go to the top of those cliffs over there and we should get a good view of the sea,' he casually suggested. The children responded eagerly and on arrival he tried to explain to them what he had in mind. 'Daddy loves you both and wants to do what is best for you, but I can't do my work properly and look after you too,' he explained. 'Now each of you take one of my hands and we will all jump together.' As they got nearer the edge and peered down the steep high cliffs, the children became very frightened and began to scream and cry. A passer-by rushed up to the distraught father, pointed to the notice board and offered to phone the church. On hearing that the pastor would be there in a few minutes, the father consented to wait and talk with him.

After listening to his sad story, Mr Emi invited all three of them to get in his car and go back to the manse where they could talk more leisurely. After consulting his wife, Mr Emi kindly offered temporarily to look after the children until such time as the father could make better arrangements. The offer was gladly accepted and that evening he returned to Osaka with a much lighter heart.

For a time monthly support came for the children but when my wife and I visited Mr and Mrs Emi in 1981 they told us that they had received nothing for two years! They did not know where the father was now living and they had no means of contacting the mother. The children had come to look upon the Emis as their parents and quite innocently the little girl said to Mrs Emi one day, 'Don't grow old!' 'What do you mean?' asked Mrs Emi, 'we all grow old.' 'We want you always to be our Mummy and Daddy,' was the reply!

Some years earlier Mr and Mrs Emi, having no children of their own, had adopted an unfortunate girl when she was 12 years of age. She was now married and had a child of her own, so the Emis were already grandparents and now quite unexpectedly had been called upon to bring up two young children. Mrs Emi is disabled and walks with the aid of a crutch, so doubtless this new demand upon her has been a very real challenge. During the war she broke her leg and unfortunately it was never set properly, for it was a time when good medical aid was not easy to obtain. As I listened to this moving story, I found myself asking whether I would have been willing to bring up someone else's children in that way and could not help but admire them for what they were doing. It helped me to realise something of the cost of the ministry in which they were engaged with its many unexpected demands upon their time, energy and patience. Would-be suicides cannot be fobbed off with a brief five minutes counselling session, but often long hours have to be spent listening to depressing stories of other people's troubles. Calls may come at the most awkward times and can not be ignored or postponed.

Mr Emi has earned the respect of many of the local poeple. As we purchased some fruit, he turned to the shopkeeper and introduced me saying, 'This is an English gentleman.' Pointing to Mr Emi, the shopkeeper replied, 'And this is a Japanese gentleman!' We were entertained to lunch at a local restaurant and as Mr Emi went to pay the bill the lady at the desk waved him past saying, 'I can't accept money from someone doing such self-sacrificial and noble work as you.' Mr Emi thanked her and tried to make a joke of it by replying, 'You should have told me that earlier and I would have eaten a lot more!'

Through this work Mr Emi has become widely known throughout Japan and enquiries come from far and near. He has been interviewed on television, various newspaper articles have been written about his work and he has written two books, which have had a wide circulation.

When I visited Shirahama in 1987 Mr Emi was able to inform me that the mother of the children had been traced. She had broken off her relationship with the other man, had returned to Osaka and was now looking after her children. The whereabouts of the father was not known. During the school holidays the children love to come to Shirahama and stay with the Emis, for they look upon it as their second home.

'Do you continue to get frequent calls for help?' I asked Mr Emi. 'Almost daily,' was the reply, 'in fact I was called out at three o'clock this morning to help a lady who was on the brink of suicide and spent one and a half hours counselling her.' He went on to inform me that he knew of fifty-seven who had been converted through his 'suicide ministry,' one of whom is now the pastor of a church and another is studying for the ministry.

The young worker, of whom at one time I almost despaired, has become in the hands of the Master Jeweller a precious gem and He had unearthed the rough stone from the seclusion of a Buddhist Temple. Along the coast at Wakayama prefecture there are several lighthouses, flashing their warning to the passing ships. Likewise this other jewel seeks to radiate His light and flash warnings to those who are in danger of wrecking their lives, pointing them to the One who said, 'Whoever follows Me will never walk in darkness, but will have the light of life' (John 8:12).

Jewel No 2

The Grandmother who was an Intercessor

It was a warm summer's evening and the oppressive humid heat had not yet begun. Earlier in the day Mrs Machida had looked after her young grandson, having carried him on her back. She was becoming very much aware of his increasing weight and was not sorry to return him to his parents. She lived alone and had gone home to prepare her simple evening meal of fish, grilled over a little charcoal fire, rice and vegetables. After slowly drinking green tea, she had done the washing up and then went for a short walk.

As she slowly walked along the bank of the river, she looked across at the little harbour. Fishermen were unloading fish from their boats and on the horizon she could see other fishing boats returning.

There was only a handful of shops in the section of the town of Susami in which she lived. As she proceeded along the main street, she passed her brother's hardware shop and then heard the sound of singing. Her curiosity was aroused and so she ambled along to see what was happening. The Christians were holding a small open air meeting. Her younger brother and his

wife sometimes attended their services, so she decided to listen
to what they had to say. As she stood listening, a lady of her own
age approached her. 'Would you like to come to the evening
service immediately after the open air meeting?' she politely
enquired. 'Oh, no,' replied Mrs Machida. 'I am much too shy to
go to the foreigners' home.' 'There is no need to be shy, all are
welcome there.' 'Well, as a matter of fact, I have always been
a bit inquisitive to know just what they do teach. If you will take
me, I will come.'

Somewhat nervously she accompanied Mrs Matsuda.
Stepping out of her *zōri* (sandals), she climbed the steep step at
the entrance of the house. There were about twenty people,
mostly middle aged women, seated on the *zabuton* (cushions).
As unobtrusively as possible she sat down on one of the vacant
zabuton. The foreigner's wife, who had not been at the open air
meeting because of putting her two young children to bed,
politely bowed to her and bade her welcome. The tunes of the
hymns were unfamiliar, but the singing was hearty and so she
tried to join in. She did not fully understand the sermon but was
impressed by the earnestness and sincerity of the young Japanese pastor. She later discovered that the pastor and the missionary usually took turns in preaching and she found the Japanese
pastor easier to understand!

The following morning she visited her brother's shop. 'I
hear that you were at the Christian church yesterday evening,'
he remarked. 'Yes, Mrs Matsuda invited me to go.' 'Onesan
[honourable elder sister], what are you trying to become - an
authority on comparative religions? Did you not go to the
Konkokyō Church for twenty years, the Tenrikyō Church for
ten years and now you have started on Christianity!'

Yes, it was true, Mrs Machida had been seeking for thirty
years through other religions something that would meet the

deepest needs of her heart. Left a widow after barely three years of married life with two small children to bring up single handed, hers had not been an easy life. She had become a school teacher in order to support her young family. Now the children were grown up and life had become somewhat easier. She was 54 and a young grandmother.

Having broken the ice by attending one of the Christian services, Mrs Machida began coming regularly on Sunday evenings. After her conversion, she amused us as she testified one evening, 'I started with the Sunday evening services and then made a nuisance of myself by attending the morning services too'!

The excavation of this jewel had taken many years but the process of grinding and polishing proceeded quickly. Her spiritual growth was rapid, although she was not young. Perhaps the secret lay in the fact that she grew in an atmosphere of prayer.

About this time the Japanese pastor voiced to me his burden saying, 'I will never be satisfied until there is an early morning prayer meeting.' 'Why don't the two of us begin?' I suggested and so Mr Adachi and I started meeting for prayer at 6 a.m. on Susami's stony beach. We met on the beach at first because we had two small children who were light sleepers, but with the advent of the colder weather, we met in the rented house which was serving as the church and our home. Later some of the Christians began to attend, amongst them Mrs Machida and her close friend Mrs Nagano. They were always on time and would quietly wait outside in the cold if I happened to be a few minutes late opening the doors!

The Lord blessed the work in the little town of Susami. The Christians were becoming more mature and steadily advancing towards self support. The time had come for the work to be handed over to Japanese leadership and for us to move elsewhere.

During the years that followed the Christians first purchased a central plot of land and eventually erected their own church building. After so much prayer, sacrifice and effort, the dedication of that simple building was indeed a day of rejoicing for that little flock.

Thirteen years after leaving Susami I was happy to accept an invitation to speak at a weekend of services in the new church building. Turning to the pastor, I enquired 'Do you still have early morning prayer meetings?' 'Yes,' was the reply, 'We continue the pattern that was established in your day. We still meet at 6 a.m. five mornings each week.' 'Do Mrs Machida and Mrs Nagano still come?' I further asked. 'They have rarely missed,' stated the pastor. What faithful intercessors they have been!

As they have knelt in prayer those precious jewels have absorbed and reflected the beauty of the Light of the World, the Lord Jesus Himself. Perhaps the blessing upon the work has come more in response to their prayers than to the sermons of the preachers. Did not Alfred Lord Tennyson in his immortal poem *Morte d'Arthur* once write, 'More things are wrought by prayer than this world dreams of'?

More than thirty years have elapsed since Mrs Machida became a Christian. Throughout those years she has faithfully and wholeheartedly supported all of the activities of Susami Church and is still a very valued member.

Jewel No 3

The Gangster whom Christ arrested

The Minatogawa Market consists of masses of little shops with alleys running between them. It is known as the cheapest shopping area for food in Kobe. The shopkeepers vie with one another to sell their fruit, vegetables, fish, meat and other items. The narrow thoroughfares are crowded with shoppers bustling with one another. At such busy seasons as immediately before the New Year, it is so crowded that shoppers need great patience.

Mr Yamashita and I were walking along together one day in that vicinity. He pointed to a spot near the entrance to the market and said, 'Two were killed there one night when a rival gang attacked us!' Rolling up his sleeves he pointed to some of the scars on his arms, reminders of the awful life that he had led as a gangster. 'It's a miracle that I was never inside a prison,' he added. 'I have nineteen gunshot and knife wounds in my body as constant reminders of the kind of life from which the Lord has saved me,' he further informed me.

As a child he had run wild and caused his parents many a heartache. As he grew older the pranks became more sinister and he gradually drifted into a life of crime. The friends he chose were equally bad for he began to associate with gangsters. One of the dangers in joining such an association is not only that of confrontation with the police but the difficulty of ever getting free again. Once a member of a certain group of gangsters, always a member - is the recognised creed. There are only two acceptable means of escape - the payment to the leader of a very large sum of money or to cut off your little finger and hand that to the leader. Drastic steps are often taken against members who try to escape by some other route.

For many years the Japan Evangelistic Band has operated a mission hall in the heart of Kobe's red light district. It was the vision of one of the founders, Mr A. Paget Wilkes. His vision became a reality through the generous gift of a Canadian supporter. At the back of the mission hall there was a labyrinth of narrow streets in which the majority of the buildings were gambling dens, drinking places or immoral establishments. In the subdued lighting would sit heavily painted young ladies trying to entice the passers-by, some of the more brazen of them would literally try to pull in young men from off the street. From other buildings emanated raucous singing by those whose throats had been well lubricated! From yet other buildings could be heard the shuffling of the mahjong ivory pieces as the gamblers bent over the tables.

Surely this is unlikely soil in which to dig for precious jewels? 'The Lord's ways are not our ways.' From amongst the rubble and hard rock, He has unearthed many a rare gem through the years. The policy of the JEB has been to encourage the converts, when numerous enough and mature enough, to form their own church in another part of the city. Then the work begins all over again. This has been done several times through the years and a number of churches has resulted. From amongst the converts about seventy have later trained in our bible college and gone into full time Christian service. The work, though tough, has not been without its encouragements.

It is doubtful whether there is any church in Japan which reaches with the gospel so many 'first timers' and amongst those who are 'fished in' off the street are those who come from all walks of life, including many drunks! Frequent are the interruptions and occasionally an inebriate has to be escorted from the building in order that the service can continue. Some of our more burly students are employed in this difficult task and I remember one man, who was the worse for drink, resisting arrest! He grabbed the front bench which fell back with a crash, hitting the bench behind it and a whole row of benches went down like a stack of dominoes!

The open air meetings are a feature of the work. These are held three nights of the week all the year round regardless of the weather. There is a pedestrian thoroughfare in front of the hall up and down which thousands of people pass daily.

As Mr Yamashita walked up that thoroughfare one evening, an unusual spectacle confronted him. A group of young men and women stood in a circle facing the mission hall. Some had tambourines, one was playing an accordion and two had drums. Several times they sang 'What a friend we have in Jesus.' He was impressed by the testimonies that these young people gave to the change in their lives since they had come to believe in the Lord Jesus Christ. An older man mounted the box and spoke very earnestly for about ten minutes and, although Mr Yamashita did not understand all that was said, he did understand that there was a service to follow in the hall to which all were invited and it was *nyōjo muryō* (entrance free). A number of people surged forward and he joined them.

As he sat listening to the message that evening there was born within his heart a desire to be different and to give up his present mode of life. The Holy Spirit convicted him of the wicked life that he was then living, and an appeal was made at the end of the service for any who wanted to be saved to remain behind for counselling. The young evangelist who talked with him afterwards spoke very quickly and related some of his own experiences. Mr Yamashita was even more deeply convicted of his need to repent and to accept the Lord Jesus Christ as his own personal Saviour. A struggle was going on within his heart as he faced up to what it might cost him to follow Christ. What would his fellow gangsters say? Would they not laugh him to scorn? What action would they take against him? How would he be able to earn a living? How could he make retribution to those he had wronged? If he made a decision, how long would he be able to keep it up? These were some of the questions revolving in his mind. Mr Yamashita, however, was not a man to be easily deflected once his mind was made up. Quickly reaching a decision, he fished in his pocket and, to the bewilderment of the young evangelist who was counselling him, handed over his revolver, saying, 'Look, I want to be saved tonight. I want to start a new life. I am going to give you this revolver to let you see that I am in earnest.'

That evening the Lord created another jewel out of the most unlikely material. Mr Yamashita became a scrap merchant and faithfully followed the Lord until his dying days. His only daughter was baptised in the same mission hall many years later.

Jewel No 4

The Maid who built a Church

The congregation at a Free Methodist church in Osaka listened attentively to the powerful sermon that was being preached that evening. The Rev. Oda, a pastor with a wealth of experience, sensed that the Lord was speaking especially to some hearts and, as he brought his message to a climax, he made an appeal.

Amongst those who responded was Miss Imagawa, a middle-aged lady whose life had been a hard and difficult one. She was poorly dressed and her dentures were ill fitting, certainly not one to attract attention for 'man looks at the outward appearance but the Lord looks at the heart.' He saw the potential of this life if dedicated to Him. Her whole life had been a struggle with poverty, particularly during the years immediately after World War II. She and her elderly mother lived in a rented room in the village of Taeji, which was about half an hour by electric train from the city of Osaka. She does not remember her father for he died while still quite young - another of alcohol's victims!

After counselling her and explaining clearly the way of salvation, Pastor Oda nearly frightened her out of her wits with his challenge 'Now you must go back to your village and tell everyone that you have become a Christian!' What a thing to ask of a new born babe in Christ! 'How do you expect me to do that?' she meekly enquired. 'Well, I tell you what I will do to help you. I have got an old drum in the back of the church and I'll lend you that drum. You can go around the village, beating the drum and telling everyone that you have become a Christian!' Would you have picked up the drum? I don't think I would, much less have gone around the village beating it! Simple soul that she was, Miss Imagawa did pick up the drum and in that way very literally nailed her colours to the mast!

There was a hunger in her heart to know more about the Christian faith, but it was an expense to go regularly to church in Osaka, so she seized the opportunity of visiting quite frequently Mr and Mrs Bee, who were living in the nearby town of Furuichi. She sought to time her visits to coincide with the hour when she anticipated that they would be holding family prayers, for she was keen to study the Word of God. If she was invited to choose a hymn, it was always the same - 'The old rugged cross.'

Realising how poor she was, Mrs Bee thoughtfully suggested to me that I might help by giving Miss Imagawa my mending to do. One of my shirts was mended so many times that it finished up almost with more patches than original material!

At the end of family prayers one day, she turned to Mr and Mrs Bee and said, 'How about coming to my village one day and telling the boys and girls and the adults about the Lord Jesus Christ?' 'We would be only too happy to do so,' replied Mr Bee, 'but where would you hold the meetings?' 'You can meet in my home,' was her immediate reply. 'Do you think that would be big enough?' asked Mr Bee. 'Oh, yes, the people in my village don't know much about Christianity, so I don't suppose many would come,' she answered. The choice of the day was an unfortunate one, for it turned bitterly cold on that February day and the snow was falling quite heavily as we went around the village, beating the drum in an endeavour to round up the children. Miss Imagawa and her mother lived in just one room which measured 12' x 9' and contained several large pieces of old fashioned furniture. Her expectations were far exceeded that afternoon for more than a hundred children tried to crowd into that room, and I was amongst the forty or so who failed! We stood outside in the snow and listened to a Japanese pastor telling the children the story of the prodigal son! But what happened to the elderly mother? As she saw that horde of children advancing on her one-room home, she took fright, disappeared into a cupboard and never reappeared until the last child had gone home!

In the evening in the same room thirty-three adults gathered to listen to a simple presentation of the gospel. I am happy to relate that before the final summons came, the elderly mother had made her peace with God by accepting the Lord Jesus Christ into her heart and life as personal Saviour.

After the death of her mother, Miss Imagawa became a maid in the home of a wealthy Japanese family and had to work long hours from early morning till late at night. There were three generations of the one family living under the same roof - the grandparents, the parents and the grown up children and each of the generations had to have different meals prepared!

If you had stood outside that large wooden house at 7 o'clock on a Sunday morning, you would have seen a poorly dressed little lady emerging. Where was she going? To the nearest railway station to catch trains that would take her on a two hour journey back to her native village. What was the purpose of her journey? To teach a handful of children about the Lord Jesus. Why was she poorly dressed? Was she not receiving a fair salary? Yes, she was but she had the vision of a church building in her village, so nearly every yen that she earned was going into her church building fund! A farmer gave her a small plot of land and a carpenter built an inexpensive little wooden church. You might be excused if you had referred to it as a wooden hut but I wonder whether any lofty cathedral was more precious in His sight. It was my privilege one Sunday afternoon to be present at a service to dedicate to the Lord the little wooden church, which had been erected through her vision and largely through her savings.

On her day off she would sometimes visit us although we lived some thirty miles from where she was working. She would arrive without warning, expecting to stay the night and would be away the following morning at the crack of dawn after quickly eating her favourite breakfast - a bowl of porridge! Our thoughtlessness once caused her a sleepless night! When we left Susami the Christians kindly presented us with a nice Westminster chimes clock, which strikes every quarter of an hour. Unfortunately it was in the room in which Miss Imagawa was trying to sleep and we had forgotten to switch off the chimes! The following morning quite innocently we asked, 'Did you sleep well?' 'No,' she truthfully replied, 'that wretched clock kept me awake all night!'

At the time of one of her visits she told me that they were going to have prize-giving at her Sunday school. 'Three of the children have only missed three times each during the whole of the past year,' she informed me. 'Isn't that wonderful?' she exclaimed. 'It is,' I said looking down at her, for she was only about half my height, 'and how many times did you miss?' I enquired, realising what it cost her in time and money each Sunday to make that two-hour train journey each way. Bashfully she lowered her head and replied, 'By the grace of God, I didn't miss once.' She doesn't have the benefit of much education, but such ability and knowledge as she possesses are wholly dedicated to the Lord's service.

'If I can gather some of my former Sunday school children for a meeting, will you come and speak to them?' she enquired one day. 'With pleasure,' I replied. It was only a small group that met in the home of a Christian doctor but, after a meal of rice curry, it was my privilege to address those young people. Amongst them was a student from Osaka University, who was studying to become a dentist, and another student from Todai, Japan's number one university - the Oxford or Cambridge of Japan. They had both become Christians and they used to attend her Sunday school.

After her retirement Miss Imagawa went to live in the little wooden church. There was no running water and no electricity, but there was no place where she would have been happier. It was the House of God and her Palace.

If you visited that same site today, you would not find the little wooden church. It has been demolished and in its place stands a two-storied reinforced concrete building. The Lutherans have taken over the work, so that Miss Imagawa now resides downstairs and the services are held on the upper floor.

'I rarely have to buy anything these days, for the Lord supplies all of my needs,' she confided to my wife. True enough I had never seen her so smartly dressed before, but she had not bought those clothes for they had been given to her. As Mrs Bee once remarked, 'I never expect to see Miss Imagawa in heaven, for she will be much too near the throne for me to see her!'

God 'chose the lowly things of this world and the despised things . . . so that no one may boast before Him.' Does not her dedication to the Lord challenge us to ask ourselves how fully are our lives dedicated to His Service?

Jewel No 5

Is there Life after Death?

Summer days in Japan can be exceedingly hot and humid, so the shallow river beds with occasional deep pools of cooling water are a great attraction for most children in the holidays. Alas, these can be places of tragedy too!

Komurasaki was a happy fifteen year old in his final year of middle school. Soon he would be a high school student and in a further three years from now, he looked forward to getting a job in order to help financially his widowed mother and his younger brother, to whom he was deeply attached. A bright summer's day often follows the downpours of the rainy season, welcome to both the rice-growing farmer and the dry stony river beds.

'Little Brother', who was nine years of age, decided that it was just too hot to stay indoors any longer. The electric fan had been whirring incessantly but had failed to cool him down. Endless cups of cool barley tea didn't seem to help much either . . . no, the best remedy in this heat was to go and jump in the river!

The family will never know exactly what did happen after that fateful decision to go for a swim for, when they next saw Little Brother, he was lying lifeless on the river bank as other boys sought frantically to revive him with artificial respiration. The silent, seemingly harmless, river had robbed him of the precious gift of life.

How could such a thing have happened? Why has he been taken from us? We all loved him so much. Where has he gone? Will we ever see him again? What endless questions filled their hearts as they struggled to come to terms with the awful tragedy that had come so suddenly on such a lovely summer's day. Such a shock takes a long time to overcome - if ever.

A broken-hearted mother and two older brothers decided that something must be done to comfort and console the soul of Little Brother. A pilgrimage to the island of Shodo and its eighty-eight temples was one of the traditional ways of earning rest for the departed soul of a loved one and so it was decided that Komurasaki should go on a pilgrimage. Donning a white robe and wearing a wide-brimmed straw hat, he picked up his pilgrim's staff and made his way to the ship at Kobe harbour that would take him to Shodo Island. It would mean a lot of tiring walking and long distances on foot as he went from temple to shrine but surely this would bring some comfort to the soul of his younger brother. He paused briefly at each successive Buddhist temple or Shinto shrine to offer a prayer for the peace and repose of his beloved brother.

On graduating from high school three years later, Komurasaki obtained employment with the Kanebo Cosmetics Company in Kobe. Accommodation was provided in the company hostel and, as he was walking between the station and the hostel on his return from work one day, his attention was drawn to a tent being pitched on a piece of ground nearby. His curiosity aroused he discovered that a Christian tent mission was shortly to commence. Well, perhaps he would go along one evening and find out what it was all about. The meeting was not particularly well attended but the enthusiastic singing and the earnestness of the preacher certainly compensated for that. Somewhere deep inside the heart of Komurasaki a need was awakened and, even though he didn't go back a second time to the meetings, yet a seed had been sown in his heart.

He decided to buy a bible from the Covenanter Bookshop in Kobe and in doing so received an invitation to attend their English bible class. In that way he met Mr Setoyama, a police liaison officer and a member of this class, who, on hearing that Komurasaki was living at Suzurandai, told him of our English bible class on Saturday evenings in the community hall. And thus it was that he not only found his way to the English bible classes but through them to the Sunday services. His was a heart prepared to respond to the claims of the Lord Jesus Christ upon his life and in the bible he found positive answers to the questions of life after death and the destiny of the soul. The triumphant resurrection of the Lord Jesus gave to all the hope of a glorious future and this life was but a brief prelude to what lay ahead. Eagerly he grasped the chance of spending eternity with Christ and decided to follow the Lord.

With verve and enthusiasm he threw himself into the church activities in Suzurandai, helping in every way possible - with Sunday school, duplicating the weekly church bulletins, distributing tracts and invitations to the meetings and in many other little ways - becoming a valuable helper to the young pastor in charge there. Being blessed with a cheerful and gentle manner, he soon endeared himself to all at the church.

Not very long afterwards he was confronted by a severe test. Was he prepared to accept from the Lord the call to full-time service and give up his present occupation? In Japan the family system is strong and important decisions are often made not so much by individuals as by the whole family, so he had to discuss this possibility with his family. Immediately he encountered opposition from both his widowed mother and his elder brother. On hearing that it would involve four years of training, his mother nearly had a fit and exclaimed, 'Why give up a well paid job for one that seems to offer such poor remuneration?' His brother was even more aggressive, 'What's the matter with you?' he exploded. 'Have you got some idealistic notion that you are going to become some great saint? Are you unhappy in your present job?' he enquired and then kindly offered without waiting for an answer to his questions, 'Would you like me to set you up in business on your own?' Mr Komurasaki explained that he was not concerned about earning or making a lot of money for a change had come into his life and thinking since becoming a Christian. He felt an obligation to share with others the good news which had brought peace and joy to his own heart, and in view of this he wanted to go to the JEB Bible College to train to become a full-time Christian worker. 'Become a Christian pastor and live on the gifts of other people? That's like becoming a beggar!' sneered his brother in disgust.

Like so many other students who have come to us for training, Mr Komurasaki did so in the face of strong family opposition. Four years later he graduated and was appointed to our mission station of Shido in the island of Shikoku, a work which had been started some years earlier by Miss Margaret Marcks, one of our American lady missionaries.

Obedience in the Christian life is often difficult and may involve going against the wishes of those who are nearest and dearest to us. There is the difficult choice between hurting their feelings and doing what we believe to be the will of the Lord - a choice that many a missionary candidate has had to face! Obedience may involve suffering and sacrifice but we have our Lord's own example for 'He became obedient unto death, even the death of the cross' (Phil. 2:8), and we can learn from Mr Komurasaki's experience that it pays to obey the Lord.

The first person he ever baptised was his widowed mother, who had opposed his going to bible college! She had come to believe that Jesus Christ was indeed the Son of God and her personal Saviour, but there was one obstacle to her being baptised - the numerous family idols. After a lengthy conversation with her son, she agreed to their destruction and Mr Komurasaki sought the cooperation of his elder brother who, although not a Christian, agreed to help smash up all of the idols. Together they loaded the broken pieces into a truck and dumped them in the sea near to the city of Akashi on the inland sea.

Sad to relate the mother did not live long after her baptism. I wrote a letter of sympathy to Mr Komurasaki and the acknowledgment contained a sentence which I shall long remember - 'Since my dear mother went to be with the Lord, heaven has seemed so much closer to me.' Yes, there is a life after death and it pays to obey the Lord!

Mr Komurasaki went on to become the pastor of the Hanoura Church where they had their own church building and adequate living accommodation for him, his wife and their five children, but his heart was very much in pioneer evangelism. A fresh challenge came to him in the form of a call to the work at Shirakawadai, a fast growing housing estate on the outskirts of Kobe. Again it demanded sacrifice and this time the choice was perhaps more difficult for it involved not only himself but also his wife and children. At Shirakawadai there was no church building and their large family would be very cramped in the small rented bungalow, but he and his wife have taken up their crosses and have risen to the challenge of this large housing estate with its unlimited possibilities for outreach.

Jewel No 6

The Man who honoured the Lord's Day

'If all Christians were strictly to observe the Lord's Day, how much more evidence there would be of the Lord's hand at work and how much more would we Christians be blessed' so wrote Ichiro Goto more than ten years ago.

Remembering the sabbath day, to keep it holy (Exo. 20:8), had not been easy for him. Like so many other Japanese, his employment involved working on Sundays. How many Christians have had to wrestle with this difficult problem! Mr Goto's determination to put the Lord first resulted in the loss of several jobs, but how wonderfully the Lord has rewarded the faith and obedience of His servant.

At the time of his conversion he was working in a solicitor's office, having graduated in law from university. It grieved him that some Sunday mornings he was unable to attend church, due to the pressure of work. Shortly afterwards the pastor of the church, of which he had become a member, invited him to become a Sunday school teacher. This involved regular attendance each Sunday morning. As a result, not only were his wages reduced but those in the same office began to complain. After much prayer, he gave in his notice and joined another company.

During the course of the interview he requested permission to attend church on Sundays. The head of the company was understanding and granted this concession, but his fellow employees were not so understanding. They accused him of being a shirker and pointed out that none of them enjoyed working on Sundays. Rather than compromise, Mr Goto resigned. Mindful of the sacrifice that the Good Shepherd had made for him, he took seriously his responsibility to 'feed His lambs' in the Sunday school.

What should he do now? As he was living on his own, it was essential that he find employment quickly in order to pay the rent for his apartment. Having studied law at university, he had been given responsible jobs in the companies for which he had worked. Consequently he found himself often deprived of adequate time to prepare the Sunday school lessons and he realised that unless he put the Lord first, he was not fit to be a Sunday school teacher.

On learning that the head of a large company was looking for a chauffeur for his private car, although not a job where his training would be utilised, he applied for the position. He got on very well with his employer who trusted him implicitly. 'You are a good man who neither drinks nor smokes. Would you like to sign a contract to work for my company for the rest of your life? I'll pay you whatever you feel is right,' offered his employer one day. He was pleased by such an offer but did not feel that he wanted to spend his life in this way, so did not sign the contract. He enjoyed driving the beautiful car and was quite happy to help the son with his school work.

However, one day this man boasted that he had twenty-eight women besides his wife. He began to feel that although the job was an easy one and the pay good, it was not right to work for such an immoral man, so he prayed daily for guidance.

He was one of a family of seven, five children and his parents, and there were many other relatives, but he was the only Christian. This was a constant burden on his heart. About that time, however, he had the great joy of seeing his younger brother become a Christian. Then one of Japan's leading evangelists, the Rev. Koji Honda, came to Kobe for a gospel crusade. At one of the meetings the Lord spoke to him through Isaiah 6:8, 'Whom shall I send and who will go for us?' He went forward to consecrate his life to the Lord for full time service. This involved going to bible college, a course which was strongly opposed by both relatives and friends.

On hearing of his eldest son's intention, his father was absolutely furious. He raved at him and pointed out how much he had spent to put him through university. He then turned on his wife. 'What do you mean by bearing me such a foolish son?' he angrily berated her. 'Not a penny will you get from me to go to any bible college,' he promised his son. The parents were keen supporters of a religion known as *Meshiyakyō*. 'As our eldest son, it is your duty to look after the financial needs of your parents when they are elderly. Oh, why were you born such a bad boy?' he continued.

His mother was more sympathetic and eventually agreed to help with his bible college expenses.

Each Monday, his free day, he made a point of visiting his parents in an endeavour to win them for Christ. It involved a thirty-mile journey on his motor-cycle but faithfully each successive Monday he visited them and sought to share the gospel with them. They did not listen very willingly to what he had to say and sometimes he was ordered out of the house. Eventually, however, his persistence had its reward. On his 150th visit they promised to attend the gospel crusade at Kobe, which was being conducted by the Rev. Koji Honda.

His heart leapt for joy when, to his amazement, he saw both his parents and his sister go forward in response to Mr Honda's appeal. With tears in their eyes they repented of their sins and asked the Lord Jesus to save them. To be honest, he had not expected such an early response for they had always been so obstinate in refuting all his arguments. Prayer had prevailed.

The most unpopular of his many relatives was one of his aunts. Miraculously enough she was converted soon after his parents. Further thrilling events were to follow for, in quick succession, a brother, a sister and another aunt all became Christians. His parents and one sister were all baptised on 19 December 1971.

Blessing, too, came to the Sunday school. He had been discouraged because, in spite of his strenuous efforts, he could not raise the attendance above thirty children. New children would come for a few Sundays and then stop coming. About this time numbers began to increase and in a comparatively short time there was an average attendance of a hundred on Sundays. It became necessary to run two Sunday schools.

In spite of his studies at the bible college, he devoted a lot of his time to his Sunday school children. He loved to paint and painted a whole series of *kamishibai* bible stories. The word *kamishibai* really means 'paper theatre.' A wooden frame in the form of a theatre stage is used. The storyteller slots in a succession of pictures with which he relates the story. He used to go with the children on picnics or took them swimming, winning their confidence and affection.

One Sunday afternoon we invited him to come to our home for a special children's meeting. The light partitions between our living room and dining room were removed and more than seventy children squatted on the *tatami* (straw) matting. It was very much a 'one man show'! Mr Goto led the meeting, played the organ and spoke to the children! In spite of the crowded conditions, he had no difficulty in holding the children's rapt attention. You could have heard a pin drop as they listened wide-mouthed!

In the words of his own testimony - 'I am just a humble servant of the Lord, but He has rewarded a hundredfold my faithful observance of Sunday as the Lord's Day. I can only thank the Lord for the joy I find in living. As I walk along the streets near my apartment, many children come running to me. They hold my hands and walk by my side.'

His father, who was saved at the age of 63, was the chief engineer of a ship which transported Japanese cars to various countries of the world. Three members of the crew were saved through his father's testimony.

His mother was a seamstress and ran a high-class dress-making business, employing some thirty young ladies. Sunday was their busiest day but, after becoming a Christian, she not only closed on Sundays but every Thursday morning set aside time for prayer and bible study for her employees. Regular house meetings were held each week in the Goto home and these were very well attended by neighbours and friends. Mr and Mrs Goto burnt their expensive *Butsudana* (Buddhist altar) and threw the ashes in the nearby river.

All of his sisters and his brother have become Christians. Two of his sisters married Christians and one sister and his only brother followed their elder brother's example by training at the JEB Bible College. On graduating his brother became the pastor of a church in Hokkaido, the northernmost of Japan's four main islands. His sister joined the JEB and worked with Miss Maureen Smith in a church planting ministry at Oasa in the island of Shikoku. When Miss Smith returned to England, Miss Goto became the worker in charge. It had not been easy for her to enter bible college at the age of 32, an age when many young ladies are becoming desperate about marriage but the Lord is blessing and using her at Oasa.

Mr Goto himself is the pastor of a growing church at Nagoya, Japan's third largest city, and he has a growing family too for already there are eight children. He loves the Lord Jesus and he loves children.

In I Samuel 2:30 can be found this precious promise, 'Those who honour me I will honour'. Mr Goto, who sought to honour the Lord's Day and who made personal sacrifice in an endeavour to win for Christ the children under his care, has certainly proved the truth of that promise.

Jewel No 7

The proud Mayor who was humbled

Mr Hatanaka was a proud man and rather reserved - proud of his academic background and of his subsequent achievements. Unlike today, when nearly all young Japanese people strive to gain admission to university, it was only the fortunate few who enjoyed that privilege when he was young. It was during his student days that he first came into contact with Christian teaching through attending the English bible class of Mr Parrot, a British missionary. His sole reason for attending was to improve his knowledge of the English language, for he was ambitious and eager to gain rapid promotion in his chosen profession of banking. An improved knowledge of English would surely be an asset, he decided.

His appointment as manager of a bank at Susami led to higher ambitions, for there were those who suggested to him that he should stand in the forthcoming election for mayor of the town. As mayor he was hardly a social success for he did not find it easy to mix with other people, but preferred his own company and a quiet family life. Social functions, a necessary part of his new appointment, were endured rather than enjoyed, but Mr Hatanaka was a conscientious person and the welfare of the residents of the town was very much on his heart.

It was a time when so many of the young people were leaving the rural areas to go to the cities to provide the workforce for Japan's expanding industries. Mr Hatanaka was well aware of some of the dangers of this and was keen to retain as many of the young people as possible. He was fighting a losing battle, for the prospects in the cities were so much better. Two of his pet projects were the hospital and the nursery school.

He was able to get a hospital started in Susami, which served a number of the neighbouring towns. At that time tuberculosis was rife in Japan and many of the patients were long-term ones suffering from that dread disease. He also started a nursery school to enable more of the young mothers to take up some form of employment. Both of these projects provided additional jobs for a number of the local people.

Shortly after arrival at Susami my Japanese colleague and I paid a courtesy call on the mayor. He received us politely, told us of his student days and of his attendance at an English bible class. He enthused about his hospital and his nursery school.

After some years as mayor, Mr Hatanaka became more ambitious. He stood for election to the senate of Wakayama Prefecture and he fought a vigorous campaign in which he was wholeheartedly supported by his wife and daughters. He toured the district in an open vehicle, with election slogans plastered all over it and one of his daughters spoke through the loudspeaker urging people to vote for her father. Mr Hatanaka somewhat self-consciously waved to the people in the streets. The Hatanaka home was a hive of activity with supporters coming and going all through the day and late into the night. Mrs Hatanaka and her daughters were kept busy serving green tea and light refreshments and as the election neared its climax Mr Hatanaka was feeling exhausted, but was buoyed up by the enthusiasm of his supporters.

On the evening of the election day an excited crowd gathered at his home. As the evening wore on, however, instead of becoming noisier those present grew quieter for the early results were anything but encouraging. The atmosphere became more and more depressing and when the results were finally announced, they learnt that their candidate had done very badly. In fact he was one from bottom in the poll. After quietly expressing sympathy, the supporters dispersed in stony silence.

It was a big blow to Mr Hatanaka's ambitions and pride. In order to stand for the prefecture, he had resigned as mayor so he was now without a job, and suitable employment for a middle-aged man was not easily found. He returned to banking.

It so happened that the house which we were renting was next door to the Hatanakas. Our house served as both our residence and the church and a narrow public footpath separated the two houses, both of which looked out on the beautiful bay. The Hatanaka house stood close to the mouth of the river and on the opposite bank was the entrance to the little harbour which sheltered about 150 fishing boats. Well maintained and newly painted they were an impressive sight.

One morning my Japanese colleague had come to our home for prayer and discussion about the work. As he looked out of the window Mr Hatanaka chanced to pass. 'Unless that uncle's nose comes down a peg or two, he will never get saved!' remarked Mr Adachi. Mrs Hatanaka used to come to many of our services and her daughters sometimes came too when they were home, but never the proud ex-mayor!

However, two events conspired together to turn his footsteps in our direction. He always seemed to feel tired and became somewhat alarmed when the doctor informed him that he was suffering from high blood pressure and needed to be careful. He became so worried that much of his time was spent in bed and he only went for gentle walks along the sea front.

It so happened that we had arranged to hold our first convention at Susami about that time. We had invited as our speaker the Rev. I. Ojima, chairman of the Church of Jesus Christ in Japan group of churches and a highly respected lecturer for many years at the JEB Bible College. We needed accommodation for Mr Ojima and approached the Hatanakas, who kindly agreed that he should sleep at their house and come to us for meals. Mr Ojima was able to have some helpful talks with Mr Hatanaka, who, to our great surprise, came to all of the meetings. He suggested to Mr Hatanaka that he should read two pages of the bible each day - a suggestion which was followed very faithfully during the ensuing weeks.

After the convention had ended Mr Hatanaka started coming regularly to our Sunday morning services. We had no chairs for like most Japanese homes there were thick straw mats, known as *tatami*, on the floor. The people sat on *zabuton* (cushions). Mr Hatanaka at first was very reserved and self-conscious and used to sit on his cushion like a statue. If, in the course of a sermon, a humorous remark was made, not a flicker of a smile would cross his face! In fact, if others laughed he looked somewhat reproachfully at them! My colleague felt quite inhibited when preaching in front of him! As soon as the service was over, Mr Hatanaka politely bowed and then made a quick exit!

However, the big 'thaw' gradually set in, the reserve and the air of superiority began to melt. The ex-mayor was even seen to half smile at some humorous remarks, although usually checking himself half-way! He began to stop for a few minutes after the services and talk with others, becoming much more relaxed and at home, sometimes stopping to thank and talk with the preacher.

In Japan Christmas Day is a normal working day. Instead they observe the New Year. The first three days of January are national holidays. As a consequence the churches usually hold their special Christmas services on the Sunday before Christmas Day, unless December 25th is a Sunday. The evening service is normally an informal one. One Christmas at Susami we began with a candlelight service at which a number of carols were sung and a brief message was given. An informal circle was then formed and refreshments served. Inevitably personal introductions had to be made going in turn right round the circle. Everyone knew everyone else, so introductions were hardly necessary, but it is a good old Japanese custom! It helps to break the ice and loosens some tongues! Invariably some laughs result. At the conclusion of the meeting four people were invited to say a few words by way of personal testimony. One of those invited was Mr Hatanaka. With surprising agility he sprung to his feet, stood on his *zabuton* and gave a most moving testimony. He confessed to having been very proud but told how the Lord had humbled him. First through ill health and then through the bible, the Lord had showed him the wretchedness of his sinful heart. He had come to understand how insignificant we are in the sight of an Almighty God and how the Lord hated pride. He believed that the Lord Jesus Christ was the Son of God and now lived within his heart. He asked those present to pray for him and to help him to become a good Christian.

Jewel No 8

Thankful for TB!

Mr Sugimoto lay on his hospital bed and stared up at the ceiling. What cruel fate had landed him in this position, he wondered. He was 30 years of age, and had already been a patient for several years in two different hospitals. After World War II many people in Japan contracted tuberculosis. His mind went back to 8 December 1941 - the fateful day on which Japan had entered the terrible second World War.

At that time he was a member of the crew of a naval vessel that was sent on operations to one of the islands of the Southern Seas. As they were about to land the soldiers, they encountered enemy ships with a cruiser as their leader. Fighting continued for the space of three or four hours. Their ship was fortunate enough to escape with light damage and they succeeded in completing landing operations.

'I was wearing a "thousand stitch belt" and there were more than thirty lucky charms hanging from my waist,' admitted Mr Sugimoto. Fear had led most of his friends superstitiously to adopt similar adornments. 'When shells were falling on various parts of the ship, I lost confidence in my special belt and other lucky charms,' he added. 'I felt that somewhere there must be a real God and prayed earnestly to Him for safety and

55

protection. Whether or not it was in answer to my prayers, I do not know, but although frequently in danger I was brought safely through the War.'

After the War he joined the merchant navy and travelled to various parts of the world. It was at that time he became unwell necessitating a return to Japan, and it came as a terrible shock to him to learn that he was yet another victim of the dreaded disease of tuberculosis.

He had a high temperature, was feeling physically weak, and had difficulty in walking. 'There is an ancient saying that one never recovers from TB, so I became very depressed. It's all up! I shan't live much longer!' he said to himself. The doctor must have read his thoughts for he advised him, 'Never let sickness beat you, Mr Sugimoto, you must win through!' The advice was heeded and, as he thought of the words of the doctor, Mr Sugimoto resolved that he would not die but would fight this disease.

One day he was visited by a follower of Tenrikyo. 'Join us,' he urged him. 'If you believe the way we do, you will soon be healed,' he promised. 'Like a drowning man clutching at a straw I joined them, but there was no improvement in my health,' related Mr Sugimoto.

Thoughts of death continued to trouble him and he began to doubt the very existence of God. 'If there is a God, why did you take my father and mother so young? Why did you smite me with TB?' he asked. There were no answers to his questions and he cursed the very name of God.

At that time, seemingly quite by accident, he turned on the radio. He had tuned in to a short Christian broadcast, he enjoyed the singing and was impressed by the speaker. He discovered that this was a regular weekly programme and, as he listened week by week, the words of the preacher gave him fresh hope.

Peace came to his heart, his health improved and he felt altogether happier. As yet he did not know the Lord Jesus Christ as his own personal Saviour, but it was at that time that he was transferred to the hospital at Susami.

There was a gentle knock at the door. Mr Sugimoto raised himself on one elbow as a young nurse entered. 'Sugimoto San, the head doctor wants to see you right away.' Quickly slipping out of bed, he donned a dressing gown and made his way downstairs. On entering the room he found that the head doctor had two guests, a Japanese colleague and myself. They were paying a courtesy call on the head doctor in the hope of being able to start services for the patients.

Dr Tamura was by no means a typical Japanese and was in his late forties. He was keen on sports although not athletic in appearance! He was diabetic and a chain smoker, so quickly tired when playing baseball with other staff members! He wasted little time in informing us that he was a communist and an atheist! 'Chances of starting meetings here are pretty remote,' I said to myself as he talked with us. But I was wrong, for he went on to add, 'You are quite welcome to come to my hospital and hold services for the patients. Furthermore, I will encourage my wife and two sons to go to your church services, but don't expect to see me!' He was true to his word and about eighteen months after the start of the work we held our first baptismal service in the sea at Susami. Amongst the fifteen who were baptised were Dr Tamura's wife and four patients from the hospital.

After introducing us, Dr Tamura turned to Mr Sugimoto and said, 'These Christian teachers have asked permission to start services for the patients. I don't see any objections, do you?' Mr Sugimoto nodded agreement. 'Don't think I am opening the door to every quack sect that wants to gain an entrance and I don't want Tenrikyo or any of these other healing religions coming along here and upsetting the patients,' he warned. Mr Sugimoto little realised that the commencement of these services would change the whole course of his life.

From the beginning the weekly services were well attended. Many of the patients welcomed the diversion and enjoyed the singing. The Holy Spirit worked in some hearts and one after another was converted. Mr Sugimoto came regularly and was usually on hand to welcome us on arrival.

One Sunday afternoon four of the patients were going for a short stroll together. 'Let's call on the Christian teachers,' suggested Mr Sugimoto. We sat on cushions around the low table talking and drinking green tea. Suddenly my Japanese colleague jumped to his feet and grabbing Mr Sugimoto by the arm, said to him, 'Come into the next room, will you? I want to talk to you.' As they talked together Mr Sugimoto made the greatest of all decisions, he accepted the Lord Jesus Christ as his own personal Saviour.

Mr Sugimoto's conversion came as a great encouragement to my Japanese co-worker, who was passing through a time of acute personal crisis. His whole future was hanging very much in the balance. As he shared with me his innermost feelings, I became deeply troubled. We had enjoyed a happy working relationship and his enthusiasm had been an inspiration. It was largely through his initiative and enterprise that the work in the area had developed so rapidly for he was a most conscientious and devoted worker. As he confided some of his failings and misgivings, I asked him, 'Have you ever trusted the Lord to sanctify you and fill you with the Holy Spirit?' He was silent for a few moments and then replied, 'To be perfectly honest, I know the theory in my head but have never had the experience in my heart.' I urged him to seek the Lord. A few days later we were seated at a low table eating our breakfast when he looked up with a cheerful and peaceful expression on his face. 'I can't put it into words,' he said, 'but the Lord has just given me peace about the future and the assurance that He has cleansed and filled my heart.' We bowed our heads in prayer and thanked the Lord.

The most remarkable thing to me was Mr Sugimoto's conversion the very next day. During the four months that we had worked together my colleague had not spared himself in an endeavour to spread the gospel and develop the work, but he had not led a single soul to Christ. The day after he had trusted the Lord to sanctify him and fill him with the Holy Spirit, he had the great joy and privilege of leading Mr Sugimoto to Christ.

From that time onwards Mr Sugimoto became our chief contact in our work at the hospital. He often accompanied us as we visited in the wards and he was able to persuade some of the patients to confide in us and to share some of their problems. His knowledge of the patients enabled him to give us wise advice and counsel.

Some of the patients had individual rooms and problems arose which the head doctor had not foreseen when the hospital was constructed. Many of the patients were bored and were vulnerable to the attractions of the opposite sex. Immoral relationships developed and more than one patient was prematurely discharged. Some of those attending our services succumbed to such temptations and one of them, a married man with two children, was deeply convicted of his sin and confided in Mr Sugimoto, who asked permission to share this with me. It was largely, I feel, through our brother's discretion and careful handling of this case, that this man was brought to repentance and was restored to the Lord. Unfortunately the woman involved hardened her heart and never really repented, but went on to get involved with other patients.

Mr Sugimoto spent no less than ten years in hospital. You might say ten of the best years of his life. On eventual discharge he took up residence in Susami and became an active member of the church. He married one of the Christians, became a *yoshi* and changed his name to Sugahara.

In Japan some families, where there are daughters but no sons, will either adopt a son or arrange for one of their daughters to retain her name on marrying. In such cases it is the husband who takes his wife's name; such husbands are known as *yoshi* and it saves the wife's family name from dying out. Comparatively few Japanese men, however, are willing to become a *yoshi*.

The Lord blessed the marriage. Mr Sugahara has a small printing and duplicating business, his wife runs a stationer's shop and they have two children. He is the senior deacon of the church and a great help to the pastor.

When asked to write his testimony it contained the sentence 'I thank God for having contracted TB. Otherwise I might never have heard the gospel of the Lord Jesus Christ.' Ten years is a very long period to spend in a hospital, but it proved to be on the one hand the soil from which the gem was unearthed and on the other the grinding process which polished it.

Jewel No 9

Prayer that recovered a Plough

Farms in Japan are very small and Americans sometimes refer to them as 'pocket handkerchief' farms. The main crop is rice and it is amazing how much they manage to produce. In the southern parts of Japan most farmers are able to have two crops per year. No sooner has the barley or the wheat harvest been reaped, than they will be busy with their ploughs preparing the ground for the next crop. Having completed the ploughing the fields will be irrigated and they seek to utilise as much of their mountainous country as possible for agriculture. Skilfully they manage to divert the water from little mountain streams to flood their fields and then the young rice plants will be transplanted. It is an unenviable task and a back-breaking one to plant the rice in neat little rows. For centuries it was all done by hand and it is only in recent years that there has been some degree of mechanisation. I have a lovely slide which was taken a few years ago. It depicts two farmers standing on opposite banks. Each is holding one end of the string, so the plants will all be placed in straight rows. In between stand about fifteen women ankle deep in mud and water. They are doing all the hard work of transplanting the young rice plants, while the gallant men hold the string! How true it is that the life of a woman in a country where the gospel has long been proclaimed is so much easier than that of her less privileged sister who has been brought up in a non-Christian environment.

Failure of a crop in pre-war Japan often had very sad consequences for the farmer and his family. They usually had large families making it a very real struggle to feed and clothe their children, and it was by no means uncommon for a farmer to sell one of his daughters to a brothel keeper to help pay his debts. She would, through no fault of her own, find herself condemned to the unpleasant and degrading life of a prostitute.

The small Iwamoto farm was located near to the southern border of Susami and the railway line ran alongside it. Their house was small but it was home for ten members of the family - the parents, six children and the grandparents.

At the time that we commenced work at Susami, their eldest child was 17 years of age. He was in his third and final year at Kushimoto High School and early each morning he boarded the train, taking a packed lunch with him. The journey from Susami to Kushimoto took exactly one hour. During that time the train wound its way along the beautiful coast and passed through no less than thirty different tunnels, giving some idea as to how mountainous is that part of Japan. He was a bright and intelligent boy and easily the most competent in English of those who came on Saturday evenings to my all too large English bible class. It was a great disappointment to us when, on graduating from high school, he moved to Tokyo to work for the Nōmura Shōten KK. This is a constant problem in church planting in rural areas for, on graduating from high school, so many of the most promising young people move to the cities to go to university or to take up employment.

The eldest daughter, Keiko, did not have the same interest in English as her brother but derived greater pleasure from our services, becoming a Christian and was one of the first group to be baptised. She later took up nursing and moved to Osaka, Japan's second largest city, but we were grieved to learn that she was no longer attending church. Young converts face many temptations and distractions when they leave their homes and go to the big cities. As I jostled with the crowd at an Osaka baseball stadium in October 1980 at the conclusion of one of the Billy Graham crusade meetings, I heard a voice calling 'Heywood Sensei!' I turned but did not recognise the person who was calling, for it was more than twenty years since last we met. Keiko gladdened my heart as she related how she had come back to the Lord, was attending church regularly and her husband had become a Christian. To me, it was like a refreshing drink of cold water to a thirsty soul. 'Cast your bread upon the waters; for you shall find it after many days.' (Eccl. 11:1)

The service had usually begun when Mrs Iwamoto slipped in as unobtrusively as possible and sat on one of the *zabuton* (cushions) at the rear of the room in which our services were first started. She was little encouragement to me in those early days! As I was doing my best to preach in the difficult Japanese language, I would look at her sun bronzed face and watch the old head beginning to nod! Is there anything more discouraging for a preacher than to see people falling asleep? However, I had a good deal of sympathy for Mrs Iwamoto, for I knew that throughout the day she would have worked in the fields alongside her husband, doing hard manual work. At the end of the day she would have gone home to prepare the evening meal for her large family and, after tidying up, she would have rushed along to the Sunday evening service. No wonder she felt sleepy! It is to her credit that she continued to come although she found it hard to understand much of what she heard. She had a hungry heart and although at times discouraged, and finding little at home to encourage her, she continued to seek she knew not what.

Mrs Iwamoto continued to attend many of the Sunday evening meetings but was unable to come on Sunday mornings. Her husband would not consent to her 'wasting' her time in that way. She requested that her daughter Keiko might be baptised but admitted that she herself was not yet ready to take such a step.

One morning she came to the back of our house and she was obviously in great distress but declined the invitation to come inside, saying that she could only stay a few moments. She had come to ask for prayer for they had purchased a new plough which for them constituted a considerable investment. The previous day they had used it to plough up one of their paddy fields finding it so much easier to use than their old plough which was really worn out. At the end of the day they had gone home tired after a full day's ploughing and, after a bath and the evening meal, they had retired early to bed. The following morning they were up at the crack of dawn and, after a hurried but substantial breakfast, set off for the fields. They were shocked and dismayed to find that the plough was not where they had left it. They searched high and low but failed to recover the stolen plough. 'I am off to the church to ask for prayer,' announced Mrs Iwamoto, 'Don't stay away too long,' her husband called after her.

After listening to her distressing story, we bowed our heads where we stood in the little courtyard at the back of our home. We asked the Lord to restore the plough after which Mrs Iwamoto quickly excused herself and set off for home. As I entered the house Miss Okahisa, who was helping us in the home prior to entering the JEB Bible College as a student, turned to me and said 'What an extraordinary thing!' She made no attempt to conceal that she had listened to the conversation with Mrs Iwamoto! 'What do you mean?' I asked. 'Do you remember the passage of scripture that we studied at family prayers a few minutes ago?' she enquired. 'Yes,' I replied. It was II Kings 6:1-7 - the story of the recovery of the lost axe head in the days of Elisha. 'Do you think that the "stick" (v.6) might stand for prayer?' she suggested. 'That's an excellent idea,' I said and the two of us had a further word of prayer for the recovery of the lost plough.

At that time we used to have an early morning prayer meeting five mornings each week, commencing at 6 a.m. The number one item on the prayer agenda for successive mornings was the recovery of the Iwamoto plough and at the mid-week prayer meeting on the Wednesday evening too, many and earnest were the prayers that were offered for the plough. Nothing happened and we felt so powerless and ineffective! Here were we proclaiming an Almighty God who loved to hear and answer prayer, but quite unable to demonstrate the truth of what we taught! To make matters worse, the farmer said to his wife, 'If those Christians can pray back my plough, I'll become a Christian!' Why was it that the prophet Elisha in a pre-Christian era without all the aids to faith that we enjoy, could simply cut down a branch of a tree, throw it into the river Jordan, and up came the lost axe head; whereas we, with all our advantages, were unable to recover the plough?

About ten days had elapsed. The early morning prayer meeting had ended and the handful of Christians, who had attended it, had returned to their respective homes. It was about 7 a.m. when Mrs Iwamoto slid back our back gate and called out 'Gomen kudasai' (excuse me). Her expression was more cheerful than on the occasion of her previous visit! 'The plough's back!' she exclaimed. 'Praise the Lord, tell me what happened,'

I requested. 'We found it in a pit not far from the field from which it was taken,' she explained. 'Why didn't you look there before?' I asked, half scolding her. 'Of course we looked there before,' she replied indignantly. 'The Lord has answered prayer. The thief has been convicted and has restored our plough,' she added. We bowed our heads and thanked the Lord. This very evident answer to prayer was a great encouragement to our small group of Christians. Sad to say the farmer never made good his promise and he died without becoming a Christian.

Mrs Iwamoto's faith was greatly strenghtened and in due course she confessed the Lord in baptism, becoming a steadfast and reliable member of the Susami church. Hers has not been an easy life, but her faith has enabled her the better to cope with various adversities.

Jewel No 10

The Gambler at Wits' End Corner

Uwajima is a fishing port on the west coast of the island of Shikoku, famous for its feudal castle and for bullfighting! No, not the Spanish type of bullfighting, for the contest is not between toreador and bull, but bull is pitted against bull.

The annual festival is held in August and crowds come from far and near to watch the contests. Fortunes are lost and won as bets are placed upon the contestants. It more resembles Sumo wrestling than the traditional bullfighting. The young bulls are marched into the ring and induced to meet head on. The winner is the bull that pushes his opponent out of the ring or causes him to fall.

Young Futagami was born in 1943 when Japan was at war and was brought up in one of the poorer homes of Uwajima. He was one of seven children so there were few luxuries to be enjoyed in his home. He felt envious of his more fortunate companions at school. Envy took root in his heart and produced the ugly fruit of theft. More than once he was caught red-handed and severely punished. On one occasion he stole a ¥500 note. His father was absolutely livid with rage when he found out. 'Bring disgrace upon the family, will you? You good for nothing thief!' he stormed at his son. He was so angry, he just could not control himself. Grabbing his son by the scruff of the neck with one hand and a rope with the other, he trussed him up like a steer at a rodeo! He was so irate that he hardly knew what he was doing. He seized a hatchet and went to strike his son. If his wife had not placed herself between them, he might well have killed his son. As it was the blow fell on his wife and the blood came spurting from her arm. The gallantry of the mother made a much deeper impression upon the young boy than the punishment of the father! Years later he was to learn of Another who took the punishment in his stead and interposed Himself on his behalf.

At the age of 17 the young lad left Uwajima to seek his fortune in the capital. He was not sorry to leave home for his had not been a very happy childhood. The bright lights of Tokyo beckoned him. He soon discovered that the streets of Tokyo were not paved with gold, that a big city can be a very unfriendly place and that fortunes are not easily made.

Finding a suitable job was not as easy as he had imagined. At so many of the places where he enquired, he found that they were only willing to take university graduates. Eventually he obtained employment at a small factory making shirts. There were about twenty other employees. He sought to do his best and showed that he was willing to tackle any job, winning the commendation of his boss. His boss was an affable person although he demanded good workmanship. Poorly finished shirts would never pass his eagle eye and he set high standards. However, he was the type of person who enjoyed a drink with the boys at the end of a day's work. He it was who introduced Futagami San to *sake* (rice wine), a potent enough drink and comparatively cheap. It has been the ruination of so many in Japan and it is reported that one third of the fatalities on the roads are caused by drunken drivers. Many Japanese carry their large bottles of *sake* with them when they go on outings. It is the custom each year in April for many to take a day off work to go 'flower viewing', to see the beautiful cherry blossoms. It is a time when *sake* flows very freely. Little groups sit around drinking. Their faces become redder and redder. At the end of the day many make their way home on very unsteady legs! *Sake* was to cause Futagami San many a headache and to lead him to the very brink of suicide.

He quickly acquired a taste for it but his meagre salary was totally inadequate to satisfy his increasing thirst. How could he supplement his income? He turned to gambling and tried in turn horse racing, cycle racing and motor boat racing without very much success. One evening he sat on his bed and turned out his wallet. After counting the notes and the few coins in his pocket, he wondered how he would hold out until the end of the month. He was bored. His feet were itching to join his friends and go on a drinking spree. How could he earn more money? He had already approached his boss and unsuccessfully asked for a rise. He was too embarrassed to ask any of his workmates for a loan. He was desperate. He just craved a drink of *sake*. Unfortunately he resorted to a means which had years earlier got him into such trouble with his father. He began to steal. He started to steal from the wallets of his workmates. He was careful not to take too much, hoping that it would not be noticed. On several occasions he worked late, explaining that he had jobs that he wanted to complete. He offered to lock up the factory when he had finished. When all had gone, he carefully selected some of the best shirts and wrapped them in a *furoshiki* (wrapping cloth). Later that evening he made his way to a pawnbroker and sold the shirts. With a guilty feeling he slowly made his way to join his friends. A few drinks quickly eased the pricks of conscience.

Futagami San had got away with it so far but he feared that a day of reckoning was rapidly approaching. Words that his father had angrily used, came back to him, 'Bring disgrace on the family, would you? You good for nothing thief.' He hated himself for his weakness. He knew that it was wrong to steal, but his whole body constantly cried out for the satisfaction that seemingly *sake* alone could give. He would have denied that he was an alcoholic but at 25 years of age he was certainly a slave of *sake*.

A desperate need called for desperate measures. He sought to enlist the help of a friend in cutting off his little finger, hoping that the missing finger would be a constant reminder not to go drinking. To think of such a thing may shock an occidental but it is not uncommon in the orient. His friend flatly refused to cooperate. Futagami San explained his present plight and eventually obtained his grudging consent to help perform the operation. They failed to cut right through the bone but a deep incision was made. To this very day Mr Futagami bears the scar of the botched attempt to amputate the little finger of his left hand. The deep incision took several weeks to heal and the bandaged finger had a sobering effect upon him. For a whole month he never went drinking *sake*.

Once the finger had healed, the craving seemed to return with increased ferocity. What was he to do? Was there no escape? He had sought advice and help from various people, but all to no avail. He concluded that there was only one way out of his present predicament - a way chosen by so many in spite of the prosperity in Japan. Buddhism teaches reincarnation - that man goes through a series of existences in the hope of eventually attaining to nirvana (enlightenment). Perhaps this teaching, which has been widespread for so many centuries, makes suicide less feared by Japanese than those who have lived in countries with a history of Christianity. Mr Futagami began to think of means to end his present miserable existence. He decided that perhaps the quickest and easiest way would be to jump in front of an express train.

Slowly and somewhat apprehensively he made his way to the nearest station. He paced up and down, trying to make up his mind. He studied the timetable and purchased a ticket for a short journey. He became increasingly agitated and, although it was a cool evening, he was covered with perspiration. 'Eh, gomen kudasai' (excuse me), he apologised as he bumped into one of the other passengers on the platform, not looking where he was going. Pulling himself together, he made his way to the far end of the platform. After a few minutes he heard the sound of the approaching train. The blatant shriek of the whistle warned people to stand clear, but Futagami San stood his ground. Summoning up all his courage, he prepared to take that final leap that would end it all. The express train drew nearer and nearer. Mr Futagami braced himself and then fears came flooding into his mind. Was there another life after death? What would happen to his soul? What would be the feelings of his family? These were some of the questions that he asked himself in rapid succession. His feet had turned to lead and he found that he was rooted to the spot where he was standing. He was nearly blown over by the force of the wind from the train as it sped past. Slowly he made his way to the barrier. The ticket collector examined his ticket and enquired, 'Changed your mind?' 'Yes,' was his gruff reply. He had no desire to talk to anyone.

As he emerged from the station, he said to himself 'What a miserable creature I am! I am not fit to live and I am afraid to die.' He walked towards the shops. In the providence of God a faithful Salvation Army woman was distributing tracts to passers-by in the street. The unhappy young man accepted one. He pulled himself together with a start as he read the opening words, 'You must be born again.' Turning on his heels, he retraced his steps and asked the young lady, 'What do these words mean? Do they mean that a young man like me, who has made a complete mess of his life, can start all over again?' 'That's exactly what they do mean, but a main street is hardly the best place to discuss it. Why don't you go to our Salvation Army Citadel and have a talk with the officer there?' she replied. He consented to do so and she gave him directions.

By mistake he knocked at the door of another church. Fortunately the elderly pastor was at home and welcomed him. He started to unburden his heart to a sympathetic listener. '*Sake* is my problem,' Mr Futagami explained. 'I have become a slave to drink and want to be free from it. Does Christianity have any answer?' he anxiously enquired. Producing from his pocket the tract which he had received a few moments ago, he went on to add, 'A young lady gave me this in the street. It says here 'You must be born again. Can you tell me what that means?' 'Christianity does indeed have the answer if you have the faith to believe in the Lord Jesus Christ,' replied the pastor. He went on to explain the difference between physical birth and spiritual birth. 'Man through sin has become separated from a holy God, but God loved this world and sent His Son, the Lord Jesus Christ, into it. His Son took the punishment of our sins and died as our substitute on the cross.' As he explained the deep significance of the cross, Mr Futagami remembered the time when his father had angrily taken the hatchet and attempted to hit him, but his mother had interposed herself between them and taken the blow instead of him. 'If man is truly sorry for his sins and will repent, then God will forgive him because His Son has already received the punishment of those sins. Then the way is open to receive the Lord Jesus Christ into our hearts. We are born again because we receive new life, spiritual life, His life, and that is eternal life,' continued the pastor. 'When Christ comes to dwell in our hearts, we receive a new power and new desires. We find ourselves wanting to please Him by doing good things and wanting to avoid displeasing Him by doing evil things. By His Spirit He can enable you to triumph over the craving to drink *sake*. He can even take the desire for it right away from you.'

Mr Futagami listened intently to all that the pastor had to say. 'I am willing to try anything,' he stated. The two men sank to their knees on the wooden floor of the church. The pastor prayed and then urged the young man to ask the Lord Jesus Christ to save him. He responded offering a simple but earnest prayer.

An instant change took place in Mr Futagami's heart. He had indeed been born again. He found that his will had been strengthened and the desire for *sake* had gone from him. He discovered that he could pass a shop selling *sake* without much difficulty and was able to refuse the many invitations from his former drinking companions. 'I'll give you a week at the most,' said one of his friends. But he was wrong, for Mr Futagami was a changed man. Through faith in the Lord Jesus Christ he had found the deliverance which he had sought in so many other directions. The change in his life thrilled him and he became an earnest supporter of the church where he had been born again. He spent much of his spare time studying the Scriptures and began to help with the Sunday school. The Lord started to speak to him about full-time service. He had a lengthy talk with his pastor who said that he would write to the Japan Evangelistic Band Bible College at Kobe and ask for application forms. After much prayer and careful consideration, Mr Futagami submitted his application together with a letter of recommendation from his pastor. He was very happy to receive notification of having been accepted, subject to a favourable interview at the college. There was, however, one big difficulty standing in his way. He had a girlfriend! The course at the Bible College was four years. Would she wait for him? Eventually and somewhat nervously he approached her. After explaining that he felt the Lord was calling him into full-time service, he asked her, 'Will you wait four years for me?' She flatly refused. He was very fond of her and it was only after much prayer that he 'took up his cross' and followed the Lord.

Thus it was that Mr Futagami came to study for four years at our bible college. He was a diligent student but never distinguished himself in the exams! He was one of the poorer students in the English classes! He was assigned to help at our central mission hall. As he gave his striking testimony at the open air meetings many stopped to listen.

At the conclusion of his four years of study he returned to Tokyo and became assistant to the pastor who had led him to the Lord a few years previously. The Lord too had gone ahead and prepared a more suitable life partner for him!

Jewel No 11

The Film Star who failed

Mr Akira Yamada did not have very happy memories of his childhood and youth. He was born shortly before Japan invaded Manchuria and grew up during the difficult years of World War II. It was a time of acute shortages when food became increasingly scarce. There was no heating in the winter at school. Sometimes they were taken for a run during class periods to warm them up. His clothes were ragged and his mother had done her best to patch them and keep them clean. In the latter years of the War there was the constant fear of air raids. He had witnessed the horrifying sight of whole rows of houses going up in flames when incendiary bombs were dropped. The wooden houses were, of course, very vulnerable and fire quickly spread. The fire services were powerless to cope with so many fires on every hand.

There were few distractions for young people. No school excursions such as his parents had enjoyed during their school days. Life was grim and serious. Television had not yet, of course, burst on the world scene. It was a very special treat when he was taken to a cinema. Perhaps because of this films had a special fascination for him. Although he did not see many films, he knew the names of most of the stars of that day and could tell you the names of most of the films in which they had appeared. His ambition was to become a film star.

On leaving school he applied for a job at the Tōei film studios. He helped with the work of shifting scenery and preparing sets. This led to his being given a job as an extra. He was a handsome young man and attracted the attention of one of the directors, who gave him a larger role. His feet were firmly placed on the bottom rungs of the ladder of success.

How proud he was when he first saw his name displayed on a hoarding outside a cinema. As his name began to appear in ever bolder letters, he became increasingly pleased with himself. His joy knew no bounds when for the first time he saw his name blazoned with red neon lights outside various cinemas. He had attained the fame that he had sought during the past few years. The rise to stardom had been more rapid than he had ever anticipated.

He began to relax and became too confident of himself. He was sometimes late arriving for rehearsals, expecting others to wait around to suit his convenience. He had a weakness and this he began to exploit as money came increasingly easily to hand. His weakness was gambling and he began to take a great interest in cycle racing. It was like a disease. Any spare moments and he was off to the cycle tracks, placing bets on the riders. Often he was at the cycle track when he should have been on set at the Tōei film company. Warnings from the directors had little effect upon him. He was drinking and gambling heavily. The red warning lights were flashing, but he ignored them. In his recklessness he placed ever bigger bets on the cycle riders, often sustaining very heavy losses. The entreaties of his unfortunate wife to mend his ways led to a number of heated scenes between them. A fall was inevitable and the blows came in quick succession. His wife divorced him, taking their young daughter with her, and the film company sacked him!

What was he to do? He had precious little money to fall back on. His brother came to his rescue with a generous offer. He had thought to take over a restaurant and offered his film star brother the post of manager. It was a good business and there were no less than six full time cooks employed in the kitchen. For a time Mr Yamada applied himself to learning the trade. He treated his staff well and enjoyed a good working relationship with them. His popularity as a film star helped to attract customers to the restaurant. In the background, however, lingered his weakness waiting to be indulged. As he became more sure of himself, he began to take off more and more time to go to the cycle-racing stadium. It was to prove to be his undoing for a second time. He got into debt. Wages were not paid on time.

Things reached a crisis one day. All six cooks came to him and handed in their resignations! Realising that he could not manage without them, and how difficult it would be to obtain trained replacements, he pleaded with them to stay. 'What's the use,' they argued, 'you are just a slave to cycle racing. We can never be sure of our pay and we expect you to be declared bankrupt any day.' Mr Yamada was in a difficult position. He argued with them, pleaded with them, and finally agreed to give up cycle racing. They eventually said that they would stay on and give him another chance to mend his ways. He tried hard to keep his promise and for six and a half weeks worked conscientiously, not going near a cycle track. The temptation grew stronger and stronger. On the forty-fifth day he surreptitiously slipped out of the restaurant and made his way to the race track. His feet were on the slippery slope once again. He lost £3 that day. It was no great loss, but he was sickened by the realisation of how weak-willed he was. He had gone back on his promise to his cooks.

One night, as he lay awake in bed, he began to think about the best way to commit suicide. Finally he fell asleep and had a dream in which he saw Christ hanging on the cross. His father had been a Seventh Day Adventist and had spoken to him from time to time about Christ. The following day, as he was walking along the street, he felt in his pocket. All that he had left was just one ten yen coin. Going to the nearest telephone booth, he picked up the directory. He was desperate. Somehow or other he had to find deliverance from his gambling habits. Where could he turn? What should he try next? Could the Christian Church help him? He thumbed through the leaves of the telephone directory and eventually found the number of a nearby church. It was a Baptist church but he had no knowledge of the different denominations. Placing his remaining ten yen coin in the slot, he nervously dialled the number. It was the pastor who answered the phone. Mr Yamada explained his problem and his longing for deliverance. The pastor listened sympathetically but interrupted him to say, 'I can't come and see you now. We are in the middle of a prayer meeting. A famous American evangelist, Dr Billy Graham, is coming to Tokyo in a few days time and this is an important preparatory prayer meeting. If you care to come to the church, I will be glad to talk with you as soon as the meeting ends.' Slowly he made his way to the church, found a seat at the back and patiently waited. When all had gone the pastor took him into his study and they had a long talk together. 'Yes, salvation is at hand. You can be delivered if you will only trust the Lord Jesus Christ,' the pastor assured him. He received a pressing invitation to the Billy Graham crusade.

Mr Yamada had been sobered by the conversation. He returned to his restaurant in a reflective mood. A few evenings later he made his way to the Budōkan, the largest hall in Tokyo. He found a seat in a gallery three floors up. The hall was well filled and he enjoyed the singing, which was being led by Cliff Barrows, with the aid of a large choir. Before Dr Billy Graham spoke he listened to the deep rich voice of George Beverley Shea as he sang 'I'd rather have Jesus than silver or gold.' Billy Graham spoke quickly but the interpreter was so good that the message came across very clearly. The Holy Spirit was convicting Mr Yamada of the sinful life which he had led and the way of salvation was simply explained. At the conclusion of his message Dr Graham appealed to people to come forward to the front of the platform no matter where they were sitting. He urged them to make this a night of decision and to receive the Lord Jesus Christ into their hearts and lives as personal Saviour and Lord. People began to move forward immediately. Mr Yamada found himself on his feet and slowly made his way from the third gallery right the way down to the platform on the ground floor. He was counselled, given literature, and urged to start attending a church near to his home. That night a wonderful transformation took place in Mr Yamada's heart and life. He had been born again and had found deliverance from the awful hold that gambling had upon him. The Lord had unearthed another jewel.

Not very long afterwards he asked his brother to find a replacement for him as manager of the restaurant. He had received an invitation from the Billy Graham Association to travel all over Japan, projecting their films. He found much pleasure in doing this and travelled extensively. At the conclusion of the showing of a film, he invariably made an appeal. In this way he had the joy of seeing many respond to his invitations to accept the Lord Jesus Christ as personal Saviour.

It was at the JEB Kobe Mission Hall that I first met Mr Yamada. He had brought one of the Billy Graham films to show to a group of pastors and Christian workers. It was not an evangelistic meeting but one quickly sensed that the Lord was greatly blessing and using our brother in this ministry. He told me that he was hoping shortly to go to a bible college in Tokyo to train for the Christian ministry.

The Rev. Akira Yamada is now the pastor of the Shioya Ichiryu Church at the town of Shioya (Tochigi Ken) in central Japan.

Jewel No 12

The young Organist and her problem Son

'Do you need someone to play your organ?' asked Mrs Ito soon
after our arrival at Susami in November 1953. She had obviously detected that neither Mr Nishi nor I possessed much
musical talent! Perhaps a word of confession is in place here! As
a boy I was sent regularly for piano lessons but, for one far more
interested in cricket and football, the daily half hour of piano
practice was a penance to be endured! My teacher was elderly
and was forced to retire through ill health, so I gladly announced
my retirement too but my mother promised to look for another
teacher. I managed to dissuade her but she warned 'You will
always regret it!' No prophet ever spoke a truer word! Whereas
neither Paderewski nor Rachmaninoff need have feared any
competition from me, yet I am sure perseverance would have
enabled me to reach a standard good enough to accompany the
hymn singing in those early pioneer days at Susami.

Alas, however, in spite of having purchased a small pedal
organ of my own, I failed to make much progress so the news
of a possible organist was indeed exciting . . . until I found out
that she was just a slip of a high-school girl aged 16!

However, the chance of being able to play this pedal organ
and the challenge of having to play at weekly services meant that

Akiko was also subjected to listening regularly to sermons and these began to 'hit home'.

The Lord was speaking to her heart, and sooner or later she had to decide whether she was prepared to accept the truth of the Word of God and become a Christian or reject it altogether.

The Yamanakas had a large house, which was fortunate, for there were five children - three girls and two boys - and their mother's parents lived with them. There was a small farm adjoining the house which enabled them to grow all their own rice.

After graduating from high school Akiko went away to Osaka for two years to study at the Free Methodist College in order to become a kindergarten teacher. Her faith was strengthened during that period and we were glad to welcome back our organist on her return to become a teacher at Susami Kindergarten.

In Japan the majority of marriages are still arranged so that parents will seek the help of a go between - usually a friend or relative - to find a suitable partner for their son or daughter. It is a big responsibility and the go between will seek to make discreet enquiries about the health, financial situation, family background and character of the individual concerned.

In the churches there are usually more young women than young men, so the arranging of marriages with Christian partners is a very real problem and one that can take up a lot of a pastor's time. At conferences or conventions they will often seek out other pastors to enquire whether there might be a suitable person in their congregation.

Akiko did not marry a Christian but her husband, Mr Kunio Mukai, whom she married on 1 May 1961, did not oppose her continued attendance of church and occasionally accompanied her. He was a bank clerk and the Lord blessed them with three children, a boy and two girls.

During his teenage years their eldest child, Hitoshi, had a minor breakdown and caused his parents deep anguish by refusing to continue his studies at high school. During a period of no less than four years he shut himself away at home and no amount of persuasion would make him go back to school. Akiko prayed desperately for a change of attitude and was supported in prayer by the members of the church. The pastor recommended contacting a farm run by the Hiruzen Lutheran Church to see if there might be a vacancy for him there but, when Hitoshi was approached, he adamantly refused saying, 'I hate Christianity!'

Naturally Akiko was deeply upset and very concerned about her son's future, especially as other religious groups were trying to persuade him to join them. One of his closest friends was a keen follower of Tenrikyo and invited him to attend one of their retreats so he decided to go, taking all his belongings with him and leaving his mother at her wits end. There was nothing that she could do except pray and it was a joy to welcome him home again a week later. After spending a whole week at the retreat, Hiroshi suddenly thought to himself, 'I was dedicated as a baby to the Lord Jesus Christ at Susami Church, so this is no place for me!'

After discussing the matter with his parents, he consented to go to the Hiruzen farm and to give it a try. It was not as unpleasant as he had feared and, settling down quite happily there, he learned not only how to look after cows but also how best to study the bible with the result that, after being away for two years, he returned home a convinced Christian and was baptised on 26 June 1983.

The change in Hitoshi's life was very marked, so much so that his father was deeply impressed. 'Well, if Christianity has made such a difference in my son's life perhaps it is time that I began to take more interest in it,' seemed to be the attitude that prompted his attendance at church with his wife Akiko. Imagine her joy as she began to see the prayers of many years bearing fruit and it was truly a time of rejoicing when twenty-nine years to the day after her own baptism, she was witness to that of her husband on 1 April 1984.

It has often been said in Japan by missionaries of long experience that they have noted time and time again that it seems to take the 'fires of affliction' to motivate people to seek the Lord. This was certainly true of Mr Mukai for not only had there been deep concern about his son but also anxiety about his own health, for he had recently had a kidney removed and there was worry over a tumour. However, he made a good recovery and the tumour was found to be not malignant, so he was happy to be back at work at the bank at Hiki.

A monthly meeting was started in the Mukai home and at one of those meetings Mr Mukai testified to the Lord's goodness to him and his family. Hitoshi is working conscientiously at a farm in Hokkaido and they are now praying for the conversion of their two daughters, Kaori and Megumi.

When I last visited Susami in March 1987 it was Mr Mukai who met me at the station and drove me to the church and the following afternoon he kindly drove me to Kushimoto for the service there. Praise God for the consistent playing and praying of his organist wife!

Jewel No 13

Through Trials to Triumph

Being the eldest of the family Masami Tamura was almost like a second mother to the baby of the family. She dearly loved her baby sister and could scarcely wait to get home from school each day so that she could play with this little one and entertain her. It was the brightest spot in the otherwise dark and dreary existence of those difficult days in her home. Suddenly, however, Masami was aware of some mysterious and secretive discussions between her financially beleaguered parents and an aunt and uncle, whom she did not know very well. She had no idea as to what was being discussed until one day on returning from school she was shocked and stunned beyond belief to find her baby sister was no longer in the home. She had been taken away as a result of an adoption deal by her childless aunt and uncle in return for financial help for her parents. They ran a bakery and had got into serious financial difficulties, so had grasped at this as a temporary solution. Poor Masami - she felt utterly betrayed and completely shattered. Could she ever trust anyone again? How could her own parents do such a thing and cause her so much heartbreak?

In one single day it seemed as if Masami's life had been turned upside down. What was the point of living? How could she ever be happy again? Despair and uncertainty filled her sad heart and questions without answers filled her mind.

Up until this time she had always freely discussed with her parents any problems and difficulties which she had, but now she felt betrayed and had lost all confidence in them. As the eldest of the family she felt that there was now no one with whom to share her problems. She was an intelligent girl and enjoyed high school studies but now even these were to come to an end, because of the financial situation of her family.

Through the introduction of an aunt she obtained employment at a factory making nylons. The factory was not far distant from her home but it was a rule of the company that all employees must live in the dormitory, so for the first time in her life she left home and experienced communal life. There were six to eight girls in each room and as all were young life should have been enjoyable, but Masami found herself unable to enter into their fun. She tended to look for some quiet corner where she could be on her own.

One evening on going for a walk she was intrigued to see a small group of people holding an open air meeting; the sincerity and evident happiness of those taking part impressed her. A tract was offered to her together with an invitation to the evening meeting which, she was surprised to discover, was being held in a tent. That evening she heard for the first time of the love of the Lord Jesus for all people.

Until that time she had trusted no one but her parents and her confidence even in them had been shaken, but now she learned that God loved her and this gave her courage in regard to facing the future. She enjoyed the singing, and the hymn 'Tell it to Jesus' quickly became a favourite. As she returned to her dormitory, it was with a lighter heart and with a different spirit she faced her work on the morrow.

At the conclusion of the tent mission a regular weekly meeting was started which Masami attended very faithfully for four months, but her friends in the dormitory gradually drew her away from the meetings. She went regularly with them to the cinema and to other places of entertainment, but the Good Shepherd had not forgotten her and was seeking the sheep that had gone astray.

Exactly twelve months after the tent mission she was out for a stroll one day and saw a poster advertising another tent mission at the same site as previously, so she resolved to go. The workers welcomed her warmly and she realised that they had been praying for her, making her feel that she had returned in response to their prayers. That evening she had a fresh meeting with the Lord Jesus, deciding to renounce the old life and begin a new one following the Lord Jesus. She began to attend the services regularly and made time each day to read her bible.

Her dormitory friends could not understand the change in her, making fun of her at first but, finding that this had little effect, tended to ignore her. God in His mercy had given a fresh start to one who had discovered that the pleasures of this world do not fully satisfy, but as yet her faith was still quite shallow and to deepen it the Lord allowed her to pass through a time of severe testing.

A swelling began to develop in the palm of her right hand. At first she paid little attention but, as it started to get bigger, she consulted a doctor. He merely diagnosed it as inflammation, but it was so painful that she was unable to continue her work and was admitted to the company's sick bay, going daily to a nearby clinic for treatment. It started in the palm of her hand but spread to her fingers and eventually her whole hand became paralysed. At the church Pastor Ukita put his hands on her hand and prayed for her healing and, whereas she was able to believe the miracles recorded in the Bible, she did not have sufficient faith to believe that the Lord would heal her. For a whole year she was off work and then an introduction was given to the university hospital. She went there with high hopes, thinking that they would surely get to the root of her trouble. Once again she was disappointed for her medical card was marked 'cause of inflammation unknown'. The company informed her that she could no longer occupy a bed in their sick bay, but must leave and return to her parents' home at Yoka.

This prompted her to stop attending the clinic and instead she sought the Lord through prayer, putting Him to the test - if He healed her, then she would believe in Him and follow Him! Looking back afterwards she realised how bold she, an insignificant creature, had been in addressing the Almighty God in such a manner. Desperate situations sometimes cause us to take desperate action but, nevertheless, God responded to her earnest prayer and her swollen and unbendable fingers began to mend. Day by day there was gradual improvement and what a relief it was to hold a pen again. Her hand returned to normal and, moreover, she became quite an expert with a crochet hook, making some very beautiful lace tablecloths in intricate designs when later she came to help us, first at Susami and further at Kobe when we moved there. She could outshine in performance any western cooking that she was taught!

This encouraging response to her prayers served to deepen her confidence in prayer, for had not the Lord demonstrated that He was alive and was prepared to answer her prayers? The first baptismal service ever conducted at Yoka was held on 28 July 1957 when Masami and two young men were baptised.

After the Lord had graciously healed her hand she began to pray, out of a sense of gratitude, that He would reveal to her how best she could serve Him. About this time Mr and Mrs Bee, who were in charge at the JEB headquarters, required some domestic help. The need was circulated amongst the JEB workers and Mr Ukita, the pastor of the Yoka church, approached Masami. 'Was this the Lord's answer to her prayers?' she asked herself and after further prayer applied for the job. Daily family prayers in Japanese were conducted by Mr and Mrs Bee for the benefit of the two girls helping at the HQ at Kobe and this, together with freedom to attend all of the services at the mission hall, deepened her faith making it a time of spiritual growth for her.

However, further trials and testings awaited her - testings of loneliness, of persecution by her family, of a broken engagement, of the lose of her first child and of her father being killed!

She came to help us at Susami in Wakayama prefecture but, in spite of the kindness of the Christians there, she was very lonely and coming from another part of Japan, as she did, found it difficult to make any deep friendships. She enjoyed the services and benefited from them, but felt lonely on the evenings when there were no meetings. However, God made the loneliness a means of blessing to her, for she turned to the Word of God for comfort and her study of the scriptures led her into a deeper relationship with the Lord.

As the only Christian in her family she was praying daily that her parents, brothers and sisters might be saved. To her disappointment they turned not to Christ but to Soka Gakkai - a recently formed sect of Buddhism which was experiencing phenomenal growth at that time. They sought to advocate a return to the teachings of Nichiren, a Buddhist priest who lived in the thirteenth century. Nichiren Daishonin, 'the true Buddha', was born in 1222 to a Japanese fisherman who had been demoted from samurai rank. At the age of 21 he engaged in religious study, travelled to Mt Hiei and other temples throughout Japan, coming to believe that he himself was the Jogyo

Bosatsu who had come to this world, in fulfilment of the prophecy in Hokekyo. Nichiren died in 1282 and his followers claimed that to him were given greater revelations than to Gautama, the founder of Buddhism. The modern leaders of Soka Gakkai were seeking to revive his teaching and were proclaiming that if whole families would join them, they would enjoy health and prosperity. Masami's family pointed out to her that the growth of Christianity in Japan had been very slow, for after a hundred years they could only claim 1 per cent of the population as followers whereas in a few short years Soka Gakkai had grown to 10 per cent of the population. They tried their best to bring pressure on her to break her connections with Christianity and join Soka Gakkai.

In the meantime we had moved from Susami to Kobe to help with the work of the central mission hall in so called 'Theatre Street'. Masami attended the services there and her former pastor at Yoka was now the evangelist in charge. She became friendly with one of the members and this led to their becoming engaged, but it was an unfortunate mistake which resulted in a good deal of heartache for her. In Japan, in Christian circles, official engagement ceremonies are often held in the churches when promises and presents are exchanged. Many of those present for the engagement ceremony felt concern for Masami as they saw how poorly her fiancé dressed, in spite of it being such an important occasion. The pastor began to institute enquiries and found that not only had her fiancé made no financial preparations for the future but was an inveterate gambler, making his profession of faith very suspect. The engagement was broken off and to Masami it seemed as though once again a dark cloud had descended upon her whole life. Uncertainty about the future was aggravated by the knowledge that we would shortly be returning to England for furlough and she had lived with us for the past four years. Once again the Lord comforted her with promises from the scriptures such as 'In all things God works for the good of those who love Him' (Rom. 8:28), and 'God is faithful; He will not let you be tempted beyond what you can bear' (1 Cor. 10:13). Her unwavering trust in the Lord was rewarded and she married a keen Christian young man with whom she has had a very happy marriage. As she looks back she is thankful for deliverance from one who was unworthy of her.

A further sorrow awaited her. She and her husband were looking forward to the arrival of their first child and, although a perfectly normal baby with a shock of black hair was born to them, unfortunately he was strangled by the umbilical cord. The parents were very upset and even now I can see Masami sobbing and howling uncontrollably as the inert baby lay beside her in his little coffin during the simple funeral service in the hospital room. The unfeeling criticism of her mother, 'This would not have happened if you had joined Soka Gakkai!' at a time when she was breaking her heart, hurt her very deeply.

It would seem that it is dangerous to question the permissive will of God's sovereignty, as the chain of events that followed would suggest. One evening as Masami was watching the local news on the television, she was shocked to learn that her father had been knocked off his motor-bike and had died shortly afterwards. In the midst of her shock and grief at this totally unexpected sad news, she recalled the words of her mother at the time of the loss of her baby son, 'This would not have happened if you had joined Soka Gakkai.' Her father had joined Soka Gakkai but it had not prevented this tragic death.

In addition to the earlier trials in the family there was the traumatic break up in her younger sister's arranged marriage. Refusing to consummate the marriage, she ran away from the hotel on the night of her wedding and nothing that anyone could do would ever persuade her to go back to her husband of one day. Such happenings can cause tremendous complications in Japanese families. So, as gold tried in the furnace of affliction, Masami has come through to burn brightly for the Lord and to be a testimony to the 'Abundant Life' she has found in the Lord Jesus.

Jewel No 14

She dreamed of the Lord's Return

Tomoko was one of the fortunate ones, for as a babe in arms she had been taken to Sunday school. Many of the children in Japan do not live near a church and, even if they do, the majority of them receive little or no encouragement to attend. On an average one church has to serve more than 19,000 people!

Sunday was a special day for Tomoko loved Sunday school and in particular enjoyed the singing. She sought to introduce many of her school friends. As a child she heard of the Lord's impending return and doubtless such teaching accounted in some measure for the dream that had such a bearing on her life.

Tomoko's father, Rev. S. Kogo, was for seven years the pastor of Kashiwara church and the services were held in their rather dark little house. From an early hour on Sundays there was a flurry of activity for, although Sunday school was not due to start until 8.30, some of the children would start arriving an hour earlier! The sliding partition doors, which divided the two rooms in which the Kogo family lived, had to be removed and the little furniture that they possessed had to be tucked away to make room for as many children as possible.

Such is the upheaval that takes place on Sunday mornings

in the homes of many Japanese workers and missionaries engaged in church planting ministry. Sunday is often a day when they cannot call their homes their own, for the church usually starts in the worker's home and normally it will take a number of years before the group is able to erect their own church building.

Tomoko was born in 1938 at Myoji in Wakayama Prefecture, near to the well known Buddhist temple at Mt Koya to which many came on a pilgrimage from far and near. It was a time of world conflict, for a year earlier her country had gone to war with China and there was a rising tide of nationalism and anti-foreign feeling. Christianity was unpopular and the position of JEB missionaries in Japan was becoming increasingly difficult, resulting in the eventual decision to withdraw. One of the missionaries was Miss Thoren, from the USA, who had been working in the neighbouring Nara Prefecture and, after her departure, the Kogo family took over the work in that area living at Shimoichi at the foot of Mt Omine.

Nara city was the capital of Japan in the eighth century, prior to the imperial family moving to Kyoto in AD 794, and to this day is a popular tourist attraction with its many historic buildings and famous tame deer. Nara prefecture is very mountainous and Tomoko's father did not spare himself in his efforts to take the gospel to as many of the towns and villages as possible, in spite of the wartime difficulties and restrictions.

One after another Japanese pastors were conscripted into the forces which, of course, added to the Rev. Kogo's responsibilities. Later they moved to Yagi, near to Kashiwara where stood one of Japan's main Shinto shrines. A vacant paint shop became their new home with the downstairs part being used for meetings and the upstairs for their living quarters. Tomoko's father was so busy and away so much that she treasured the moments that he could spare to play with her.

When she was only 3 years of age there was another move and this time to a more distant location. Her father had accepted a call to pastor the recently formed Otemachi church in Numazu city. With a population of 60,000 Numazu seemed to her a big city after the small country towns in which she had previously lived. Situated on the coast, it was in a nice part of the country and on clear days she could see the snow covered cone of Japan's highest and best known mountain, the beautiful Mt Fuji.

A number of pastors were arrested and imprisoned but, although questioned by the military police on several occasions, Mr and Mrs Kogo were never arrested. As the War increased in severity air raids became more frequent and her father was put in charge of air-raid precautions for the district in which they lived. There was fear that Numazu might be bombarded from the sea and one day bombs fell in two places near the church, killing some of their neighbours. As soon as the air-raid siren sounded Tomoko would run to the air-raid shelter as fast as her little legs would carry her. She was petrified as she heard the sound of the American B29 bombers overhead and the deafening noise of the ack-ack guns. On one occasion her mother and sister had a narrow escape, for they had only just entered the shelter when a piece of anti-aircraft shrapnel plunged into the upright of the back door through which they had just passed.

It was decided that her mother should take Tomoko, her brother and sister to her mother's parents' home at Obama on the opposite coast where they would be safer. Her father remained at Numazu but some weeks later, as things had become quieter, he was persuaded to take a few days rest to visit his family at Obama. That very night Numazu was heavily bombed and their church was one of the many building destroyed. Mr Kogo promptly returned to Numazu to try to help his church members as best he could, but homeless and without a church building there was really little that he could do so he rejoined his family. On 15 August 1945 the War came to an end but the Kogos remained on at Obama and endured the rigours of a severe winter in that cold part of Japan. Food was scarce and strictly rationed, and they had to sell items of clothing to buy food. One day a farmer gave them a large turnip and, as they had no salt, they boiled it in sea water and lived on it for several days.

In March 1946 her father moved to Kashiwara near to Osaka to try and re-start the church there, living in one room while Tomoko and the rest of her family remained at Obama. Eighteen months later they all moved to Kashiwara, by which time Tomoko was 9 years of age and this was her sixth home!

There were only a few Christians so the financial support that they could give their pastor and his family was minimal, but the Lord provided for them in many unexpected ways. There was blessing in the church, attendances were increasing and one year no less than thirty were baptised, but another dark cloud was approaching.

Tomoko was very fond of her younger sister Yoshiko and they spent much time playing together, but when Yoshiko was only 8 years of age she became very ill with tubercular meningitis. It was pitiful to hear her cries for she was in constant pain and her father was so distressed that he asked the Lord to take her to heaven. Yoshiko heard his prayer and cried out, 'No, Daddy, don't pray like that! I don't want to go to heaven!' Her health began to improve but then the headaches returned. One day she turned to her father and said, 'Daddy, I want to go to heaven now.' 'Yoshiko, do you know how you can get to heaven?' he enquired. 'I suppose if I do good things I can go,' was her reply. He explained to her that Jesus had died on the cross to save her and, after listening carefully, she asked the Lord Jesus to come into her heart and be her Saviour. Two days later she died and Tomoko was heartbroken. As she saw her sister lying peacefully in her *futon*, it looked as though she was sleeping and it was hard to realise that she would never speak again and that her playmate was gone.

During the war the JEB Kobe Mission Hall had been destroyed by bombing but in 1952 it was rebuilt and Tomoko's father became the evangelist in charge. It was a spacious building compared with their cramped little home at Kashiwara, but it was not a good area in which to bring up teenage children. The windows of their apartment looked out on a narrow dimly lit street in which the majority of the houses were brothels. In the evenings heavily painted women could be seen soliciting the men as they passed, sometimes even trying forcefully to drag them into their establishments.

Students from the JEB Bible College gained valuable practical experience by helping at the mission hall. The elderly principal of the college, Rev. Goro Sawamura, was so impressed by the way in which Mr Kogo handled and trained the students that he invited him to become the warden of the men students, so once again in March 1955 Tomoko and her family had to move. They lived in an apartment in the main building of the college, adjoining the rooms of the men students. The college is in a lovely location, situated on a hill overlooking the inland sea - a great contrast to the seedy area in which mission hall stands.

It was soon after their arrival that Tomoko had a dream which had a profound effect upon her. Just as Joseph's life was greatly affected by the dreams that he had so too was the life of Tomoko. At Sunday school and at church services she had learnt the main details of our Lord's return. She knew the parable of the ten virgins and of the sad fate of the five foolish ones who were not ready when the bridegroom came (Matthew 25:1-13), but she had never seriously faced the challenge 'You must be ready, because the Son of Man will come at an hour when you do not expect Him' (Matthew 24:44). She knew too the verses 16 and 17 of I Thessalonians Chapter 4, 'The Lord Himself will come down from heaven with a loud command, with the voice of the archangel and with the trumpet call of God, and the dead in Christ will rise first. After that, we who are still alive and are left will be caught up together with them in the clouds to meet the Lord in the air. And so we will be ever with the Lord.'

One night Tomoko dreamed about the personal return of the Lord Jesus Christ. She heard the sound of a trumpet and she saw the Lord Jesus descending from the clouds. Then an extraordinary thing happened - people suddenly became airborne and joined the Lord Jesus in the clouds! But Tomoko remained in her *futon* and in her dream she got up and ran to the adjoining room in which her parents slept. Quickly sliding back the door, she was dismayed to discover that their *futon* was empty and her parents were nowhere to be seen! Next she went to the room in which her elder brother Nobukazu slept but he was not there either! In a panic she walked along the corridor that led to the quarters of the men students who slept in bunkbeds, two to a room. She opened the doors in quick succession, only to find that all of the rooms were empty!

By this time she was really frightened and was wet with perspiration. What would happen to her now? Who would look after her? What would become of the bible college? She began to cry and then woke up.

The dream had been so real that she did not know whether the Lord had come back or whether it had been a dream, so she sprang out of her *futon* and raced to her parents' bedroom. What a relief it was to find two big bulges in their *futon* sleeping peacefully!

'So, it was only a dream after all,' she mused as she slowly made her way back to her room. It was some time before she could go to sleep again, for she kept asking herself, 'Supposing it had been true, would I have been caught up in the air or would I have been left behind?'

Tomoko could not forget her dream and several weeks later at Tarumi church at the Sunday evening service the minister made an appeal. He urged all who lacked the assurance of salvation to accept the forgiveness of their sins, which Jesus offered, and to receive Him into their hearts as personal Saviour. The first to respond that evening was Tomoko and it was largely the result of the dream.

It was good that she made this, the most important of all decisions, when she did because she did not live very long. It is true that she got married and had a lovely baby daughter, whom she and her husband decided to call Ayako. Unfortunately Tomoko had a weak heart. Like any young mother Tomoko was very proud of her little daughter and excitedly watched the various stages in her development but when she was 32 years of age and Ayako only 4, the Lord called for Tomoko. She was ready and prepared to respond to the Lord's final summons because she had heeded the Lord's warning through a dream some 17 years earlier.

Jewel No 15

A stormy Tent Mission and the Aftermath

As he served his apprenticeship as a plumber Mr Ozaki always looked forward to the day when he would have his own business and be his own boss. Eventually he managed to achieve his ambition but it involved the long train journey to Kushimoto, a small town in southern Honshu, the largest of Japan's four main islands. He took over a small plumbing business in the main street with accommodation over the shop for his family of four children. The coastal scenery around Kushimoto attracted many visitors and many came from the cities for the fishing, but immediately after the war was a difficult time for any business. Materials were in short supply so it often involved adapting worn equipment or searching around for alternative sources of supply. The profit margin was small and Mr Ozaki soon found himself in financial difficulties. The bank advanced him a loan but now he was saddled with the additional burden of paying off the interest.

With his financial problems uppermost in his mind he decided to get some fresh air and as he strolled along the sea front he was surprised to see a tent being erected. It was a warm October morning in 1954 and he went up to one of the young men to enquire the purpose of the tent. 'We are holding a tent mission and starting tomorrow evening there will be meetings each day for the next eight days - 6 o'clock for the children and 7.30 p.m. for the adults. It is open to everyone and you would be most welcome to come,' he was informed by the enthusiastic young bible college student who handed him a leaflet. Reading through the leaflet he noted that it was a Christian mission and chuckled to himself as he learnt that the main speaker would be a Mr Ushio (meaning Mr Cow's Tail!) from Maizuru. His mind went back to the days when he had attended Christian services at Osaka, so he decided to go and hear what Mr Cow's Tail had to say.

Kushimoto, lying at it does at the southernmost tip of the island of Honshu, is a very windy place. Perhaps this and the fact that so many of the inhabitants are fishermen, who are constantly battling with the elements, has resulted in a ruggedness and toughness of character in the people. Across the bay and connected by ferry is the small island of Oshima and during storms many ships shelter between Kushimoto and Oshima. A short distance away is the well known Shionomisaki lighthouse, constantly warning ships of the dangerous rocks in that vicinity.

Mr Nishi and I had started the work at Kushimoto the previous December as an outreach from Susami, where we were then living. It was about twenty-five miles south of Susami and a larger town. The steam train used to take exactly one hour, stopping at every little station and passing through no less than thirty tunnels. In the summer we were opening and shutting the windows every few minutes as we passed through a succession of tunnels.

Our first services were held in the main living room of a brand new bungalow which had been built for Mr Okano, a fisherman who was looking forward to marriage in the near future. Fishermen are those who are usually 'early to bed and early to rise,' so we felt obliged to leave his house not later than 9 p.m. There was no train until 11.30 p.m. and a station platform is not the warmest of places in the dead of winter! 'See that restaurant over there?' I asked Mr Nishi. 'I'm going in search of a hot bowl of *udon* (noodles). Would you care to join me?' This became a weekly ritual and never were there such so slow eaters, for it took us two hours to consume those bowls of *udon*. It was very much warmer in the restaurant than on the draughty station platform!

Each week on a Wednesday we used to leave Susami on the 11.19 a.m. train, taking our lunches with us. The afternoons were occupied with visiting and with an English class at the high school. After a quick evening meal at a restaurant, there would be the children's meetings and those for the adults. It would be after midnight before we got back to Susami - usually exhausted and often discouraged by the lack of response by the people at Kushimoto. A pioneer worker in Japan needs to be willing to pray, persist and plod away! It was a miracle that we never overslept on the train on the return journey! While we were on furlough Mr Emi, who replaced Mr Nishi in March 1954, confessed that on one occasion he and Mr Yoshida did in fact oversleep and had to alight at the next stop of Tanabe! It was 3.30 a.m. when they eventually arrived back at Susami!

Less than two months after the start of the work a building became available to us for rent and on 20 January 1954 we used it for the first time. It was a wet and windy day for our first meeting with a consequent small attendance, but it meant that we now had a base of our own where we could leisurely relax after the meetings before going to the station. The response was disappointing and few came to our meetings, so we planned four nights of evangelistic services remaining at Kushimoto throughout that time. In an endeavour to wake up the people to their need of the Lord Jesus Christ as Saviour we 'blitzed' the town with tracts and invitations to these special services. New people were attracted and one evening when Mr Nishi was preaching on the cross a fisherman's wife, hearing the story of the cross for the first time, left the building with tears streaming down her cheeks! After the meetings we would sit on the straw mats scattered around a charcoal brazier and leisurely talk with the people, to give them an opportunity to ask questions and to help us to get to know them better. It was essential that they should have confidence in us, especially as we were only visiting the town once a week and not residing there.

As a further endeavour to reach and win for Christ the people of Kushimoto, we planned a tent mission for the October of 1954 and it was through this that we first made contact with Mr Ozaki. The Rev. Ushio of Maizuru was the invited evangelist, an experienced worker who had been with the JEB in pre-war days after graduating from our bible college and had rejoined the JEB after the war. He was a likeable man, quite outspoken and not one to pull his punches, who had married rather late in life a wife very much younger than himself. When he approached the father and asked for his daughter's hand, he was met with a flat refusal. 'I can't afford a wedding,' objected the father, 'I have no money to help with her trousseau and furniture.' Weddings can be very costly in Japan and there is a common saying: 'Three daughters and that means bankruptcy!' but Mr Ushio was not easily to be put off and would not take 'No' for an answer. 'If need be, I'll take her naked,' he replied! He got his bride; theirs was a happy marriage and the Lord blessed them with two lovely daughters.

In addition to Mr Ushio two of the fourth-year students from the bible college were invited to come and help us. They assisted with the erection of the tent, with visitation, with the children's meetings and in many other ways. Kushimoto lived up to its reputation, for Wellington in New Zealand is not the only town which is well known for being windy! A gale buffeted our tent and the rain lashed against it. On the first night it rained heavily and the speaker had to compete with the flapping of the tent as the strong wind blew against it. This, of course, affected the attendance but Mr Ozaki was amongst those who did come. The following day the weather cleared and we were encouraged by having about eighty children and sixty adults at the two meetings. During the remainder of the tent mission we had a variety of weather, some days fine and some days wet and stormy. One night we had a struggle to keep the tent upright, but Mr Ushio bravely continued speaking as the wind lashed the tent and we occupied ourselves with banging in the tent pegs and tightening the guy ropes.

As I look back upon that tent mission many years later, there is one thing in particular for which I give thanks - the contacting of Mr Ozaki, the plumber, who was 45 years of age at that time. Night after night he came to the tent meetings and when the mission ended continued to come regularly to our weekly services. Whether he was converted during the tent mission or later, I am not quite sure, but what a gem he has proved to be through the years. Not only did he become an earnest Christian but later his wife and two of his children became Christians, all being baptised at Kushimoto. His only daughter, Sumiko, was musical and became the church organist until she married and moved to Tokyo. In addition he introduced a number of his employees to our services.

Not only we, but the bible college staff too, can thank the Lord for Mr Ozaki's conversion for many a long journey has he made at his own expense to help them with their plumbing problems. With so many students large quantities of water were required and the well often gave trouble. Usually it would be a seven-hour drive to Kobe but Mr Ozaki claims to have done it in five and a half hours. Like Jehu he is not the slowest of drivers and has paid several fines for speeding! 'What is that little black box on your dashboard?' I asked him one day as we were driving along together. 'Oh, that,' he said with a smile, 'is a device for warning of a police radar trap! I haven't been stopped once since that was installed!' He maintained that the police were quite happy for drivers to have such devices!

Each year at the beginning of May he would come up to the bible college for the annual four-day convention, bringing others with him. They would drive all through the night in order to come. Sleeping accommodation during the convention was very crowded and the men, who knew him, tried to avoid the room in which Mr Ozaki slept, for he had the reputation of being one of the loudest snorers! They would return to Kushimoto greatly blessed and helped through the messages that they had heard and through their fellowship with other Christians.

Perhaps we were a bit premature in inviting him to become a Sunday school teacher. With the children we were systematically teaching the best known Old Testament stories with the aid of the excellent teacher helps published by the Japan Sunday School Union. One day it was Mr Ozaki's turn to speak to the children and the subject was Noah and the flood. Graphically describing the flood, the incessant rain which lasted for forty days, the rising of the water and the drowning of the people, Mr Ozaki went on to relate that both Adam and Eve perished in the flood!

His business has prospered and he and his family live in much more spacious quarters than in those early days, but he has remained the same humble and loyal member of Kushimoto church. He has always been willing to cooperate and help in every possible way. After our visit in 1981 he drove my wife and me from Kushimoto to Susami for the evening service. En route he insisted on stopping for us to see a magnificent aquarium.

At Kushimoto today there is a self-supporting church with their own church building and pastor, Rev. Kuroda, reaching out to neighbouring towns and villages. One of their most faithful members is the gem that was wrested from the hard soil of that weather beaten town during the tent mission of 1954.

Jewel No 16

The Wife of a condemned War Criminal

'On Sunday I am going to preach at Kashiwa. Would you like to come with me?' The invitation was extended by Miss Irene Webster Smith, one of our senior missionaries. She had returned to Japan after the war and was living at Tokyo. Her vision was to establish a centre for work amongst university students. In a miraculous way the Lord enabled her to obtain a house with a surrounding garden in the heart of Toyko. It was the autumn of 1950, six months after she had moved into the property which she had purchased for £6,500. The ground alone is worth millions of pounds today! The building has gone and in its place stands a nine-storey student Christian centre. On the one side is Macdonalds hamburgers and on the other Mister Donut! Many university students are being reached and won for Christ through the excellent facilities there and office space has been provided for other Christian organisations. The Christian Literature Crusade has been provided with a good central location for their bookshop.

It took us nearly an hour to reach Kashiwa. Japan was at that time a poverty stricken country slowly recovering from the awful devastation of World War II. As we travelled on the crowded electric train Miss Webster Smith turned to me and said, 'Look at those spotless white shirts the men are wearing. When both soap and clothes are so scarce it just amazes me as to how their wives and mothers keep their husbands and sons looking so smart!' The Japanese may have been beaten but they had not lost their sense of personal pride.

I was in my first term at the Tokyo language school and often visited Miss Webster Smith, who lived quite near the YMCA where I had a room on the sixth floor. After the service I was introduced to a widow, Mrs Nishizawa, whose husband had recently been executed for war crimes.

Before the war Miss Webster Smith had run an orphanage at Akashi for girls, many of whom would probably have been sold into brothels but for her noble work. Amongst the many girls who were brought up in the orphanage was Noshi Chan, who later married a Mr Ito, a widower with four children, and went to live at Kashiwa. There was no Christian witness of any kind in the town, so she started a Sunday school. Some of the mothers came too, so she wrote to Miss Webster Smith and invited her to come and speak to them. After the service one of the women came up and introduced herself. 'I have accepted the Lord Jesus Christ as my own personal Saviour, but I am deeply concerned about my husband. He is in Sugamo prison and under sentence of death. Will you please go and visit him?' she earnestly begged. 'It is virtually impossible to visit anyone in that prison. The authorities are very strict indeed and just will not give permission,' replied Miss Smith. 'I am allowed to visit him for half an hour each month,' she explained. 'On my last trip I gave him a Gospel of John but he showed no interest. If you could go, he would probably listen to you. I will give up my visiting privilege for you.'

Miss Smith promised to try to get permission although she was not very optimistic. The prisoners at Sugamo had been sentenced by the International War Crimes Tribunal and security was very tight. She made a formal application to visit Nishizawa San at the legal section of GHQ. She was refused. 'No one can see the prisoner except his wife, mother or his lawyer,' she was informed. 'His wife has begged me to visit him and has even offered to give up her thirty minutes for me to do so.'

This seemed to affect the officer who was considering her request, for he consulted his superior officer. After a lengthy consultation a solution was found. 'Every condemned man has the privilege of one clemency interview with a priest or other religious official, but every precaution has to be taken. Just recently one of the wives smeared poison on the wire mesh of the interview booth. Her husband licked it off and died.' Her spirits began to lift as she was told, 'He is entitled to one religious interview, and if he chooses to see you, we can arrange it.' Some days later she received word that Nishizawa San had given his consent.

Sugamo prison is a cold-looking grey stone building. At the time it was heavily guarded. Her handbag was taken into custody and she was carefully searched. She was escorted along the corridors to the interview booth. Two American guards stood behind her and two behind the prisoner, as they talked through a wire mesh screen.

'I have seen your wife and children,' she began. 'They are well. I met your wife at a Christian service at Kashiwa. She is praying for you.' 'Yes,' replied Nishizawa San, 'she told me that she had become a Christian and she gave me a little booklet.' It gave Miss Smith the opening she was seeking, for she knew that he was referring to the Gospel of John. 'Have you read it?' she asked. 'No,' was the discouraging reply. She explained that the Lord Jesus Christ, God's only Son, had died for the sins of men and women. There was pardon for those who would believe in Him and the offer of eternal life. A place in heaven was reserved for those who would put their trust in Him. 'As many as received Him, to them gave He power to become the sons of God, even to them that believe on His name,' she quoted from the opening chapter of the Gospel of John and slowly introduced him to the all-inclusive promise of the well-known chapter 3 verse 16.

He listened with increasing interest and interrupted to ask, 'Do you mean that He could forgive my sins?' 'Yes, the promise is open to all, no matter how dark the past may have been,' she assured him. 'But you don't understand,' he objected, 'you can have no idea of the awful sins that I have committed.'

By way of reply she quoted, 'If we confess our sins, He is faithful and just to forgive our sins, and to cleanse us from all unrighteousness.' 'What must I do to obtain the forgiveness of my sins?' he asked. 'Believe in the Lord Jesus Christ and thou shalt be saved,' she replied.

As she began to pray for his salvation and asked the Lord to help him to believe the promises of God's Word, she asked if he was prepared to ask the Lord Jesus to forgive him and to save him. He nodded his head. She offered a prayer of commit-tal to Jesus Christ as Lord and Saviour which she got him to repeat after her. She was informed that her time was up, so, turning to the prisoner, she asked, 'Nishizawa San, do you believe that the Lord Jesus has saved you today?' 'Yes, I do,' he answered quietly. 'I want you to do something for me,' she requested, 'I want you to find some one person in the prison and tell him what the Lord has done for you. Will you do that?' 'I will try,' he promised.

What a relief and a joy it was for Mrs Nishizawa when she heard the good news of her husband's decision. 'I am so glad!

I have been afraid that he would die unsaved. The Lord has lifted a burden from my heart. I believe that his sins have been forgiven and that the Lord is soon going to welcome him into Heaven.' There were tears in her eyes as together they bowed their heads and thanked the Lord for His mercy and goodness.

Less than a week later Miss Smith received a phone call from GHQ asking her to report there. On arrival she was taken to meet the same colonel as she had met at the previous interview. 'Do you know a man by the name of Shibano?' he asked. 'No, I do not recall that name,' she replied. 'He is a condemned prisoner in Sugamo prison and he wants to meet you. He has asked for a clemency interview with you.'

She rejoiced at the realisation that Nishizawa San had shared his faith with a fellow prisoner. A remarkable sequence of conversions resulted. As the word was passed on, one after another the convicted war criminals in Sugamo prison asked for clemency interviews with Miss Webster Smith. The Lord used her to lead fourteen of them to Christ. Thirteen of them were later baptised by the Baptist prison chaplain.

One morning when she was having her quiet time she was suddenly overcome with a sense of the urgent need to try to secure a second interview with Nishizawa San. That same morning she went at once to the large Dai Ichi building near to the Emperor's palace, which was being used as the headquarters of the occupation forces. Her request for a further interview was refused.

Miss Webster Smith was not the kind of person who easily took 'No' for an answer! Had not the Lord impressed upon her that she was to go and see Nishizawa San? She determined to go right to the top and sought to see no less a person than the Supreme Commander, General Douglas MacArthur himself! When the Lord is in a thing, it is amazing how doors open! The man who ruled Japan at that time agreed to see her. He rose and received her graciously.

The General not only issued an order that she should be permitted to see Nishizawa San, but he provided a staff car to take her right away to the prison!

In the interview room she waited for the prisoner to be brought in. His face was radiant as he greeted her with the words, 'Only this morning I asked God to send you to see me!'

'The Lord must have spoken to me about the same time, for I had an urgent feeling that I must come and see you. It was General MacArthur himself who gave me permission to come!'

He gave her final instructions for his wife and children and his last messages to them. As they bowed their heads for a final word of prayer together, she noticed that the military policeman behind her had removed his helmet and had bowed his head.

The same guard escorted her to the prison gates. 'Are you a Christian?' she asked. 'My mother taught me to pray,' he said, 'and I used to go to Sunday school, but I haven't prayed since then. We've been watching you come in and out of the prison and we've seen the changes in the men. Would you come and talk to some of us?' A successful series of meetings with the military police was the outcome.

A final letter came from Nishizawa San thanking her for her visit. He wrote:

Mother Smith

I appreciate your sincerity and that you saw me again and gave me kind encouragement, sharing your busy time: and also thank you by the name of the Lord with the other brethren, hearing that the favour of baptism was realised by your unusual efforts.

I am living thankful days believing that I may receive salvation of the Holy Spirit on my last day, and entirely trusting in Him, that 'for me (saved by the grace of God) to live is Christ and to die is gain'.

Please give your kind direction to my family . . .

I pray your good health by the name of the Lord Jesus Christ and God the Father . . .

Yours sincerely,

A saved sinner

M. Nishizawa.

Shortly afterwards an American officer came to tell her of his last moments. 'They (Nishizawa and one of the other converts) died triumphantly,' he told her. 'When the clock struck the midnight hour, the two men came out of the inner prison, their Testaments clasped in their manacled hands. They were singing "Nearer, My God, to Thee", and back in the cells other prisoners sang "God be with you till we meet again".'

'The two men knelt on the trap door, praying and offering praise to God,' he went on. 'Their faces were radiant.'

As he concluded his moving account, he turned to Miss Smith and said, 'I would like to accept Christ, too. I would like to meet my Maker as these men did.' She had the joy of leading him to the Lord.

Others of the war criminals wrote too. A general wrote this poem, 'The call for the execution is as sweet as the voice of the angels. Now I start on the journey to the Kingdom of God.'

Although she realised that the dreaded day of her husband's execution would soon come, when the news did come, it came as a great shock to Mrs Nishizawa. How was she to bring up her sons single handed? Where would the money come from to feed and educate them were questions uppermost in her mind. Mrs Ito and the Christians at Kashiwa sought to comfort and encourage her. Miss Webster Smith's occasional visits were always eagerly anticipated, but in the spring of 1951 she went to England for furlough.

After Miss Smith's departure, which incidentally was on

the same day that General MacArthur left Japan, I was invited to go each month to Kashiwa to preach at their Sunday morning services. Amongst the members was Mrs Yanai. Her son worked at the Bank of Indo-China in Tokyo and he served as my interpreter. His knowledge of the Scriptures did not go very deep so interpretation was often difficult! However, it did afford me an opportunity of meeting Mrs Nishizawa on several occasions. Unfortunately language difficulties prevented me from communicating with her as freely as I would have liked. I admired her for the brave way in which she was seeking to cope with her difficult circumstances and for the way in which she was seeking to bring up her children.

The gem had been unearthed from the midst of suffering, sorrow and anxiety, but she had not allowed her personal grief to mask the glow of His new possession. On the contrary the reflected beams of her faith had penetrated the closed doors of a fortress-like prison. The consciences of a number of the inmates had been awakened and their hearts illuminated. Gloom and despair had been displaced by peace and hope. 'And they shall be mine,' saith the Lord of hosts, 'In that day when I make up my jewels.' (Malachi 3:17). Many shall in that day 'arise up and call her blessed.'

Jewel No 17

From Stonemason's son to Bible College Principal

The winter is cold and long in north-eastern Japan. The cold winds which blow across from Siberia bring with them heavy falls of snow. The town of Shirakawa in Fukushima Prefecture has an ancient castle and is a stronghold of Buddhism.

Mrs Ariga sought to keep the home warm in which she, her husband and their four children lived. They had been saddened by the loss of two of their children and, fearful of some further tragedy befalling the family, she earnestly endeavoured to teach her children the Buddhist sutras. Kiichi was only 3 years of age and he found the words too difficult to memorise, but his mother was very strict and often his punishment was to go without his breakfast!

During the summer there was plenty of work for Mr Ariga with the construction of dams, stone walls and roads but with the advent of winter there was little work. When Kiichi was a few years older, his father took him in the dead of winter to stand under a freezing waterfall as a penance for the naughty things he had done. Some Buddhist sects encourage such practices believing that the longer one can endure the icy water cascading down on one's body the greater the benefit.

When Kiichi was only 12 years of age he was shocked and stunned by the death of his closest friend, who was just a few months younger than himself. It seemed like the loss of a younger brother and at the funeral he kept wondering whether his friend had gone to hell. He began to ask himself what would have been his fate if it had been he who had died. He thought of the many wrong things that he had done in the past, of the money that he had stolen from his mother's purse to buy sweets, of breaking into a savings box to help buy a bicycle and of the many times that he had deceived and disobeyed his parents.

He began to seek a change of heart and rose at 4.30 a.m. to go either to the Shinto shrine or the Buddhist temple where he spent a long time repeating the same prayer over and over again.

When he was 14 years of age he received an invitation to attend a Christian church but it was refused. He could find no peace and, in spite of regular attendance at the temple and much prayer, he experienced no change of heart. He contemplated suicide and decided that to jump in front of a train would be the easiest way. He walked slowly to the railway and, after looking to see that nobody was watching, climbed over the wire fence. He waited anxiously and then heard the sound of the approaching train. Summoning up all his strength and courage he took a flying leap as the train was almost level with where he was standing, only to land in between the rails and the train passed over him without causing any injury! Bewildered he picked himself up, dusted off his clothes and silently made his way home again. Later in life he gave thanks that he was short in stature, as he remembered the incident which might so easily have ended in tragedy!

It was new year's eve, 31 December 1947, and Kiichi was going to the largest temple at Shirakawa. It was the custom for the priest to sound the temple bell 108 times - supposedly to wipe out the 108 different kinds of sin of which man was guilty. The number 108 is a significant number for Buddhism and a Buddhist rosary has 108 beads. A devout Buddhist carries a string of beads on his wrist and counts the beads one after another, repeating the formula of 'Namu-Amida-Butsu' (O save, Amidabha) for each and every bead he fumbles. On the way to the temple he met a school friend who was a Christian. 'Where are you going, Kiichi?' asked his friend. 'I am going to the temple,' replied Kiichi. 'Oh, no you are not, you are coming to church with me!' responded his friend. They began to argue and eventually started a fight! The friend, having learned jujitsu, quickly had Kiichi on his back and extracted a promise from him that he would come to church! It was a very real example of 'compelling them to come in'! Relating his testimony Mr Ariga commented, 'I was a bit like Saul on the Damascus road, for the Lord made me to do something against my will!'

By comparison with the large temple the Shirakawa church seemed small and insignificant. The church had been started by Hideo Nakamura, a Christian tailor, who had moved to Shirakawa after his home in Tokyo had been destroyed by bombing during World War II. His wife had been killed and one daughter was badly injured, but it had not embittered him and he had managed to find a house in this country town. He began to invite people to his home for Christian services. A Swedish missionary, Rev. Karl Gustaffson, had been forced to leave China when the communists came to power in 1950 but, although more than 60 years of age, he had come to Japan and preached through an interpreter at Shirakawa over a period of three years. It was through a message on the text, 'Son, be of good cheer; thy sins be forgiven thee' that Kiichi came to accept the Lord Jesus Christ as his own personal Saviour.

He went home and apologised to his parents for the many

wrong things that he had done in the past and became a very earnest Christian. So much so that his parents became quite alarmed, for he seemed to be going to church nearly every night of the week - so keen was he to learn all that he could about the bible and the Christian faith.

On returning home late one evening he found the door locked. He banged on the door but there was no answer. He continued knocking and eventually it was an irate father who came to the door. 'What do you mean by coming home at this late hour of the night?' he demanded angrily. 'I have been to church,' was the timid reply. 'If you will promise to stop going to church and give up Christianity, then I will open the door!' shouted his father. 'I can't promise you that,' pleaded Kiichi. 'Then you can stay outside,' said his father as he went off back to bed. That night Kiichi slept in a rabbit hutch! It was to be the first of many similar occasions! The Arigas kept five rabbits and so had a fairly large hutch.

When giving his testimony publicly Mr Ariga jokingly gives three reasons for being short. Firstly because when he was small he often missed his breakfast for failing to memorise the Buddhist sutras; secondly because he shrunk when his father made him stand under the freezing cold waterfall and thirdly because in his teenage years he often had to sleep in the cramped space of a rabbit hutch!

At the age of 14 he began attending a missionary's English bible class and started studying English very seriously. He went to three different classes each week! He is today one of Japan's outstanding interpreters and has interpreted for many well-known visiting preachers. He was interpreting one day for a Swedish missionary, Rev. Lars Fasten, who was preaching on Abraham being willing to sacrifice his son Isaac (Genesis 22). Mr Ariga was so moved by the message that then and there on

3 March 1954 he dedicated his whole life to the Lord. By this time he was 20 years of age. For a whole year he interpreted for Mr Lars Fasten, and the following year in April 1955 he was amongst the new students to enter the JEB Bible College.

When asked, 'How did you come to choose the JEB Bible College?' Mr Ariga replied, 'It was largely through Pastor Moriyama. He came to Kuroiso for a series of meetings and we used to meet together for prayer each morning from 4 a.m. to 6 a.m. One morning he spoke from Revelation 2:10, 'Fear none of those things which thou shalt suffer . . . be thou faithful unto death and I will give thee a crown of life.' He determined to apply to the same college as the one at which Mr Moriyama himself had trained. The Lord confirmed his decision during the annual convention at the bible college in May 1954.

During his time in bible college Mr Ariga prayed much for his family. His parents were such strong Buddhists that at times he despaired of them ever changing. About a year after commencing his studies he was overjoyed to receive a postcard from his mother. Tears came to his eyes as he read what she had written. She was writing to apologise for having persecuted him when he became a Christian and went on to relate that she had been baptised at Easter. It was the first intimation that she had become a Christian. Due to the costly railway fare he had not returned home during the vacations.

A neighbour's son had died while quite young and it had greatly upset the mother. Not only had she suffered on account of her son's death but she herself had become fearful of death. Not wishing to suffer in the same way or go to hell, Mrs Ariga had accepted an invitation to attend the special New Year meetings at the Shirakawa Christian church at which the Rev. Akira Takimoto was the invited speaker. Mrs Ariga was saved at the very first meeting that she attended. Doubtless her son's prayers had played an important part in that early decision.

At that time Mr Ariga was having his own trials. During his first year at bible college tuberculosis was diagnosed, but he had no money for medicine or medical treatment. He had used up all of his savings to help his elder sister who had been seriously ill. It was only through support from the principal's student aid fund that he had been enabled to continue his studies.

He studied late at nights and rose at 3.30 in the mornings, but he was convicted as he realised that his primary reason for doing this was to impress the other students. This caused him to seek the Lord for cleansing from indwelling sin. On 6 June 1956 the Lord gave him the assurance that he had been crucified with Christ (Gal. 2:20), that the Lord had sanctified him and filled him with the Holy Spirit. He felt a great sense of liberty and freedom in his heart.

About the same time the Lord spoke to him through Romans 8:11 and assured him that he had been healed of TB. He went back to his Christian doctor for a further examination. As the first X-rays showed no signs of TB, they were taken a second time. 'Have you been praying?' asked the doctor. 'Yes,' replied Mr Ariga, 'Well, a miracle has certainly taken place within your body, for neither of the two sets of X-rays shows any signs of TB!'

During his fourth and final year at the bible college the pastor of his home church came to visit him, to ask if he would help start a new church in a badly neglected part of Tochigi Prefecture. He promised to pray about it and, as he did so, the words: 'for their sakes' (John 17:19) came to him with such force that he felt led to accept the invitation.

The only Christians at Otawara were two middle-aged ladies but during the next four years the Lord greatly blessed his pioneer efforts in that area. During the first year fifty-three were saved and thirty-six of those were baptised. Self-support was achieved within eighteen months, a small church building was erected and by the time that he left seventy-five were coming regularly to the Sunday morning services.

On 25 May 1959 he was married at the Kobe Central Church by the Rev. Koji Honda. His wife's mother had been saved at the JEB Kobe Mission Hall before World War II and his wife had come to know the Lord Jesus as Saviour at an early age. They decided not to have a honeymoon but to take members of their family, who had come to Kobe for the wedding, to the crusade at Osaka which Dr Bob Pierce (who later founded World Vision) was conducting. During that crusade no less than seven members of their families were saved, including Mr Ariga's father, older brother and older sister! It was a very happy 'substitute honeymoon'. The Lord has done great things for their respective families and no less than fifty-three of their relatives have become Christians!

Shortly after this the Rev. Koji Honda resigned as pastor of the flourishing Kobe Central Church in order to devote himself full time to itinerant evangelism. Mr Ariga agreed to help him with one Crusade each month and was the soloist at many of the meetings. In 1962 he became full time assistant to Mr Honda and together they conducted crusades in many parts of Japan.

In 1971 he went to the USA for one year to study 'Evangelism in Depth' at Fuller Seminary. On his return to Japan he was appointed as director of that movement which became known as 'Total Mobilisation'. This entailed constant absences from home as he travelled all over Japan, seeking to help the churches with their evangelistic programmes and to encourage church members to become more active in seeking to win others for Christ.

Some four years later he was approached by the Rev. Eric W. Gosden, on behalf of the JEB and bible college directorate, as to his willingness to become the principal of the bible college. For him one of the main difficulties was that of finding a suitable successor as director of 'Total Mobilisation'. After some months of praying about this important invitation, he felt one day that the Lord was speaking to him through Isaiah 41:14-15, 'Fear not, thou worm Jacob . . . I will help thee, saith the Lord . . . Behold, I will make thee a new sharp threshing instrument having teeth.'

In April 1977 Rev. Kiichi Ariga became the new principal of the JEB Kansai Bible College at Shioya, on the outskirts of Kobe. He is only the third principal in the history of the college for his predecessors the Rev. Goro Sawamura had served for fifty years and the Rev. Shotaro Kogo for four years. Speaking at the inauguration ceremony on 12 April Mr Ariga asked, 'Who would have thought that a stonemason's son from northern Japan would have been invited to fill such an important position?' Referring to his fears at accepting such responsibility, he told of how the Lord had given him confidence through the promise of His presence, His help and that He would fit him for the task ahead (Isaiah 41:10 and 15).